THE INSPIRED SALESPERSON

Inspiring Reflections For God-Centered Sales Professionals

James McMechan

Published by RICHER Press
An Imprint of Richer Life, LLC
5710 Ogeechee Road, Suite 200-175, Savannah, Georgia 31405
www.richerlifellc.com

Cover Design: RICHER Media USA

Volume book discounts are available for groups, companies and organizations. Contact the publisher for information and order instructions.

Library of Congress Control Number: 2020943452

The Inspired Salesperson
Inspiring Reflections For God-Centered Sales Professionals

James McMechan

1. Inspiration   2. Self-Help   3. Sales
[pbk : alk. Paper]

ISBN-13: 978-1-7335693-3-0

PRINTED IN THE UNITED STATES OF AMERICA

September 2020

ACKNOWLEDGEMENTS

Special thanks to my family and my co-workers for their support of me while working on this project.

A huge thank you to all of those who welcomed me warmly into the sales profession and gave me a chance to be all that I could be. You were all a unique part of my inspiration.

A thank you to Pastor Joel Sims of Word of Life church who helped me with valuable insight into one of the reflections.

CONTENTS

CONTENTS

INTRODUCTION

Years ago, I went through a period of crisis. After years in the ministry, and reeling from a recent divorce, I was a man blindsided by God. To my surprise and shock, I had discovered that God didn't play fair with the affairs of the heart, and that realization MADE ME ANGRY. My resentment with God caused me to abandon my ministry, my church, my friends and even my family. I decided that if God could walk away, so could I. Like the prodigal son I was, I moved to a far-off land and started squandering my "riches" [which weren't that much] on an excessive lifestyle. I lost any sense of who I was. I didn't care what I did, or who I hurt. The truth is I figured that God would kill me for my unbelief --- or I would do the job for Him.

Eventually, I found myself, middle-aged, broke, unemployed, ashamed and deeply guilt-ridden. I ended up living in a skanky motel in a strange city, counting out change just to eat. About that time, I answered an ad in the paper to work at a local dealership. I had never sold anything like cars before. I soon realized that my job was basically to throw my body onto the hood of every car that wandered into the lot. I decided to chase every customer I could.

During the next few weeks and months, I became obsessed. I devoured every resource on sales I could, I began watching videos, reading books, listening to audiotapes, and studying product spec sheets. I wrote out my presentation [literally] to get it exactly right. I practiced in front of a mirror; working on closing techniques, and overcoming objections. I scrutinized every detail of my sales skill set; always refining, always practicing. When I found a new phrase I could use, I put it into my toolbox. I was a man on a mission. Sales became my religion. In short, I became a sort of "inspired" salesperson.

I also discovered something else. Namely, that there were lots of other hungry sales folks out there. Good people each one. Most of them had little or no experience in *sales*. And a lot of them were open to spiritual things. As I began to share my story with them, the whole thing developed into a sort of quasi-ministry. *Little did I know that God would use this avenue to begin to heal the deep wounds of my own heart as well as using it to help others.*

Now, to be fair, there are plenty of smart people out there who have made a fortune telling salespeople how to sell. This isn't that book. The internet is filled with all kinds of sales courses that have been written by people with better skills than me. Most of the time these sales *gods* have made great money with a concept or a word track that they teach over and over and over. The result of all that success is that these *gurus* end up thinking that they are God's gift to the sales world. And while the pitch they preach may be good, even great, these men are not better than you or me, no matter how many books or seminars they have sold or how many mansions they live in.

The purpose of this book is to share some basic reflections on sales, and to maybe invite God into the conversation. You might be surprised to learn that some of the best principles an inspired salesperson can have are found in the pages of God's Word.

There is no magic pill that will turn the average salesperson into a superstar. Frankly, it takes a desire to learn and a determination to work very hard each day, but mostly I found it takes a willingness to keep your heart in the right place. If that heart stuff happens and God shows up, then this labor of love will not have been in vain. As you read the pages that follow, my hope is that you will be inspired by a thought or a verse. Because you are the inspired salesperson.

I. YOU ARE THE INSPIRED SALESPERSON

Drive past any auto dealership anywhere, and chances are you will see thousands of balloons or steamers bobbing in the breeze. From stick figured giants waving their air-filled arms to the vibrant posters plastered on windowpanes, every business owner [manager] strives to create excitement and energy. Ads trumpet the latest sale. Mailers declare the ultimate blowout. Television spots shout huge discounts. It is no secret that creating buzz in the minds of the consumer can translate to increased sales and profit. If these kinds of things didn't work, companies wouldn't spend billions of dollars in advertising every year. All designed to draw more customers through their doors.

But the truth is that while advertising schemes can help bring bodies in, they aren't always enough to inspire sales. Too often, the owner or manufacturer blasts their product over the airwaves, only to discover that sales stayed flat. Think of all the effort that the chase for the elusive dollar can create. Most of that energy is a waste of effort, time and money. The truth is that balloons and banners don't sell products. People do. As an inspired salesperson, you do.

You are the most important asset your company possess.

Yes, you.

Organizations forget that the greatest resource they have isn't their pitch - or even their product. It's their people. It is the frontline employees who are striving every day to persuade the consumer to buy. It is the back of the house staff person that pushes a broom, adds up the receipts, orders the parts, or even stocks the shelves. Everyone on the team has a purpose and a place. Many an owner would see a much higher return on their investment if they would concentrate on developing the skills of their people, instead of paying money for commercials and internet ads.

You are the inspired salesperson.

But while owners often forget the importance of proper training and motivation, that is only half of the equation. There are lots of times when the staff fails to embrace the excitement needed to push sales to new heights. It's a two-way street. The owner can do his part to drive business to the door, but if the employees [particularly the sales staff] aren't engaged, and motivated to do their best, it won't matter how much money is spent. In short, you must want to be the inspired salesperson.

Where does that character quality come from? What makes an inspired seller?

It starts with *attitude*.

Employees who are inspired to give their very best realize very quickly that the right mindset is no easy task. In each of them,

12

there seems to be a determination, a wholehearted devotion to perfection that fills their hearts. Their constant goal is to go above and beyond – always exceeding the guest's expectations. When they make promises, they keep them. When they open their mouths, they speak truth. These inspired employees have a work ethic that begins the moment they step into their cubicle or onto the showroom floor. There is a hustle to their muscle and an obvious *pep in their step*. The passion for excellence is born in the mental approach they choose every moment of every day.

The truth is that in today's world, consumers are much smarter than we give them credit for. It doesn't take much for a customer to read an associate's mannerisms, facial expressions, and detect a lack of energy. They know if salespeople are honestly happy and they can surmise quickly when someone is just going through the motions. Frankly, in today's competitive market, companies can ill afford to lose business to their competitors, because of inept employees and unmotivated managers. The guest's experience is too valuable to waste. That reality means that every moment needs to be maximized, and every opportunity turned into a sale.

So how do we do it? How do we stay motivated and excited and energized enough to give our customers our very best?

The Bible might lend an answer – Here is what one passage says:

"Choose for yourselves this day whom you will serve, whether the gods your ancestors served beyond the Euphrates, or the gods of the Amorites, in whose l and you are living. But as for me and my household, we will serve the LORD." [Joshua 24:15 NIV]

In this passage, Joshua, the leader of the children of Israel, lays the two paths of life or death before the people. They could go back and serve the false gods of their Fathers or they could determine in their hearts to serve the Lord God Almighty.

Basically, he is telling the people that you will be what you choose to be. The person you end up becoming tomorrow will be based on the decisions of today.

It's as simple as that.

Reflect on your own experience for a moment. Chances are you have made choices in the past that are still having an impact on your life today. For example, you chose to marry someone and a child came from the relationship. Even though you might not be married to that person anymore, the son or daughter you have watched grow up is a product of a choice you made. Perhaps you chose in the past to pursue this career or that job, and that choice is still affecting who you are. The choices of where to live, or what to do, or who to be with, can create strong winds that can change the landscape of our lives permanently.

My father used to remind me that every decision has consequences. Sometimes those aftereffects are large and instant, like a tsunami. But not always is that the case. More often the small choices and decisions we make each day all the time can leave the deepest wounds or lead to the greatest joys. This is the point that Joshua was trying to set before the children of Israel. When Joshua tells them to *choose this day* – the verb tense is a continual act of a decision previously made. It is as if the prophet were telling the congregation to *keep on choosing*.

Choose God each day. Renew the choice every moment by continually choosing to follow the Lord in everything you do and say.

Here is another thought. Just take a quick moment to notice in the verse above that there are two definite acts to choosing and maintaining a commitment to all things holy. It's not just about embracing or turning to God; it was also about refusing to embrace false gods or turning from the old ways. As individuals, we are who

14

we are not just because of the positive traits we choose, [joy, love, hope, etc.] but also because of the negative ones we leave behind us [bitterness, anger, resentment].

Imagine for a moment that you are heading out to the beach for the day. The sun is shining and the waves are crashing and the smell of sand and surf tickles your nostrils. You can hardly wait to swim with the dolphins and feel the tide rush between your toes. As you think about heading over the dunes and out toward the sea, you glance down at what you might need to carry with you. Sunscreen? Check. Beach towels? Absolutely. Flotation devices? Got to have them.

But what about the over-sized suitcase filled with pajamas, underwear, and the hair dryer you brought for the trip? Or the nice suit you have tucked away for the evenings? Can't see how that might do you much good on a beach. I imagine that it wouldn't take long for you to realize that lugging those things through the sand will be more of a pain than a pleasure. Those items are probably going to stay locked up in the trunk of the car. And so, you leave it where it needs to be. Securely locked away.

Now I realize that every person has their own personal set of stresses. No one's worries are like anyone else's. You might be going through really hard times; illness, financial straits, or even having to face the consequences of being stupid. No matter. If you bring the bag of emotional boulders into work with you, it will just get in the way and slow you down. It will distract you and keep you from being your best. Too often, the temptation is to unpack those struggles in front of the very guests we are trying to win over.

When that happens, the message we want to convey gets garbled. It creates a huge disconnect with the people you want to serve. So, the bottom line is this: because attitude breeds attitude, we should be very thoughtful about the positive attributes we

15

embrace, and the negative ones we abandon. And we must daily, moment by moment commit ourselves to continually choosing the right path. In other words, even if it takes a thousand times a day, choose who you want to be. Remember, you are an inspired salesperson.

What attitudes do you need to embrace today? Maybe *"I can do all things through Christ who strengthens me."* [Phil. 4:13 NKJV] Perhaps, *"Be kind to one another."* [Eph. 4:32 NIV] Perhaps *"Fear not, for I am with you."* [Is.41:10 NKJV] Or even, *"Choose you this day, who you will serve."* [Joshua 24:15 NKJV] Whatever attitude you need to choose, DO IT.

Again, and again and again. Remember - it all begins with a choice. Just ask the balloon man blowing in the breeze in front of your store. He only wishes he had a choice.

II.   WHEN YOU SAY HELLO

"For where your treasure is, there your heart will be also." [Matt 6:21 NIV]

E ver walked into a place of business and been ignored? It happened to me the other day. I was browsing for a pair of pants in a local department store, just a few feet from the checkout counter. Gathered around the cash register were three or four associates, who must have been a having an informal meeting or something. Even though, they knew I was there, no one offered to help. No one said hello. No one even smiled. They just plain ignored me. After a couple of minutes of searching, and not finding anything, I decided that they didn't really want my business that badly and left. *Ironically, their company just filed for bankruptcy – guess now I know why.*

On the flip side, there is a local grocery store I absolutely love. The place is very clean. The staff greets me every time I walk into the door. They smile, wave and act like they are genuinely glad to have my business. They know me and my family by name. They ask about them when I am walking through the store alone. They genuinely care. I almost always purchase my groceries from them, even though other stores might have better sales or bigger discounts. I go there because of the way I am treated. Like family.

Many sales consultants forget that every good encounter with a guest begins with a great first impression. How quickly you greet a customer and the manner in which you say your first hello can make or break a future sale. In my business, we were taught to acknowledge a customer within 30 seconds of their arrival with a warm handshake, a smile, and a bit of *pep in the step*. Our owner knew that even though a lot of people might walk through his doors, an ignored customer never buys anything *I even had a manager who told me that if he ever caught me not acknowledging a customer with 100% effort*. I would be fired on the spot – no questions asked. [That is how much emphasis he placed on making the best first impression].

Over the years, I have had so many managers train on this greeting or that one, [there are lots of ways to greet a customer] and while the words they wanted used might have differed, every greeting included some basic truths. Every method included things like smiling, good eye contact, and engaging the guest with energy and enthusiasm. Many companies have a process on how they want their associates to initially engage with customers. Whatever the process is, make sure that you learn it and use it.

What is the key element to an effective greeting? Is it more about making good eye contact, or shaking the guest's hand firmly? Being helpful? Having high energy? Memorizing a script? While all those things can lend themselves to a making the customers feel good the moment they arrive – there is a place where all that right stuff begins. Every greeting must start somewhere - the Bible describes it as *heart*.

What does heart have to do with it? Inspired sales consultants know that first and foremost something inside their own heart must awaken before any hello is given. Without heart, it doesn't matter how much training you have or what word track you use. An employee can memorize all the facts in the world, or follow the process step by step, but without heart, they can still lose the sale. The truth is that if a salesperson or associate isn't committed to making each encounter they have with a customer excellent; the company will lose money and profit and time.

Think about the emphasis the Bible places on the heart. If you were to do a word search in the Bible, you might find many verses that talk about loving [engaging the Lord and others] with a WHOLE heart.

Praise the Lord! *"I will praise the Lord with my whole heart."* [Ps. 111:1 NIV]

"I entreated Your favor with my whole heart; Be merciful to me according to Your word." [Ps. 119:58 NIV]

"Then I will give them a heart to know Me, that I am the Lord; and they shall be My people, and I will be their God, for they shall return to Me with their whole heart." [Jer. 24:7 NIV]

Faith comes from the heart. Salvation comes from confessing what is in the heart. Love for God and others flows out of the heart. Everywhere you look in the Bible, the idea of heart [being fully engaged] is repeated - again and again.

Roman 10:9 says it so well:

"If you confess with your mouth the Lord Jesus and believe in your heart that God has raised Him from the dead, you will be saved."

The heart is a wonderful creation of God. Think about how often the normal heart beats a minute. With every pump of this vital organ, oxygen-filled blood flows through our bodies, providing much needed nutrients to every part of who we are. The heart beats and we breathe. The heart beats and we think. The heart beats and we sleep, run, eat, hear and in essence have our being. Without the heart's constant rhythm, we would cease to exist. That is how important the human heart is to our bodies. [My father died of cardiac arrest, so I know what happens when the heart stops beating].

Unfortunately, too many employees are just not that willing to *keep their hearts beating* for their guests. When a customer walks toward them with a question, they might view them as an interruption to their day rather than an opportunity. Whether they intend to or not, a lot of employees just seem to convey the idea that they do not like people very much. And from a company perspective, this kind of employee can be a cancer infecting other employees with the same lackluster attitude.

What about you? Where's your heart today? Do you really care about the guest in front of you, or do your mannerisms betray what is really in your heart? When a guest walks up, do you frown, act impatient, or respond with a sort of, "I wish you weren't here" kind of vibe? Check yourself. The next time you see a customer, try to get up off your butt and put your whole effort [heart] into welcoming them. Remember, you are an inspired salesperson.

The truth is that every customer deserves our absolute best. No excuses. And the principle is that it all stems from the heart.

III.   The Joy of Discovery

Jesus said, *"I praise you, Father, Lord of heaven and earth, because you have hidden these things from the wise and learned and revealed them to little children."* [Matt 11:25 NIV]

My autistic son has discovered the power of the Internet. Each time he surfs the web, a whole new world of information literally explodes in front of his eyes. Every day, he studies intently, traveling to new places, learning new concepts, and even acquiring brand new skills. As I step into our home each evening, I can see the joy in his eyes as I greet him hello and give him a hug. Sometimes he can hardly wait to share with me some random thought or idea he has stumbled across. It thrills him to no end to suggest that we take our next vacation to Florida, or go to a baseball game in Houston. The internet has opened up the world to my son. It has given him the power to dream of the things that might be. Now as you might imagine, as a father, his voyage of discovery has also made me a bit nervous. I worry a lot about what his eyes might be seeing.

21

So far, he has kept his online searches to safe sites, [thanks to the diligence of his mother]. Other than the random order of an educational video from Amazon, he hasn't gotten into too much trouble. *Thank God for parental controls and pin numbers, otherwise we might very well have a roomful of rap videos and travel films.* But my son's happiness has made me think for a moment. When did I lose the joy of discovery? Was it when I grew up and began to face the daily grind of life? Was it when I took on the responsibility of raising a family or being the bread winner? Was it when I accepted the reality that life wasn't fair or when I watched my dreams turn to ash like the pine straw in a fire pit? Somewhere along the line, I stopped having a sense of wonder about stuff. I lost the joy of discovery. What's worse is: I realize now that I am worse off for it.

The joy of discovery can take many forms. Whether it is learning how to highlight the advantages of their product against the competition, or changing the wording of a pitch to keep it vibrant, inspired sales consultants are constantly seeking to recapture the thrill of the new. The excitement of each fresh encounter has the potential to open up something they might not have known before. They view every interaction with a client as a chance to engage themselves to the task, and open up the power of discovery that is the very heartbeat of sales.

This unfounded joy isn't just a trait that inspired sellers keep for themselves; they also show their customers that same joy. Watch any master salesperson and you will see them often lead their listeners down the *discovery* path. They craft a product presentation filled with valuable information, helping the listener learn something they may not have known before. They demonstrate the product and allow their customers to handle, touch or push buttons for themselves. They want the customer to experience everything they experience and more. And when that salesperson sees the joy of discovery in the eyes of his buyer that is when he knows that every hour of preparation and practice has been worth the effort. That is when the sale can, and often does occur.

Salespeople have known this truth for years. There is an adage in the car business that says, "the feel of the wheel seals the deal." And it is true. There is no time when the customer in more engaged, more excited, or has more endorphins flowing through his system than when he is driving the car. The rush of the actual testing out of the item, of feeling the car move seamlessly around a curve, or even the smell of new leather sparks the senses. Many of my desk managers refused to even work a car deal until the client had driven the car.

The same is true of televisions or mattresses or any other tangible sale. Ever wonder why a salesperson wants you to lie down on the bed? Or try on a pair of shoes? Or why there are fitting rooms in every department store? Or why there were taster people at their little stations, handing out Dixie cups with fruit? *It is all centered in the act of discovery.*

Jesus knew the power of discovery. Jesus asked many of the people he encountered to participate in a small way before the "big" healing or the miracle became known. When Peter and his friends were fishing, it wasn't until they cast their nets on the right side of the boat, [a small act of obedience per Jesus suggestion] that they pulled in the huge amount of fish that day. When feeding the multitudes, it wasn't until the little boy gave up his lunch, [another act of obedience] that the crowds got fed. When Lazarus rose from the dead, it wasn't until the stone had been rolled away, [an act of obedience] and Lazarus responded to the Saviors voice, [an act of obedience] that the dead began living again. The woman with a sickness responded to the Savior's question of "who touched me?" – that little act of obedience became the vessel through which God's glory was displayed. The power of discovery is strengthened in the minds of everyone because one person chose to obey the words of the Savior.

Want more examples?

The walls of Jericho - the children of Israel marched and shouted [an act of obedience] and then the walls came tumbling down. Gideon and his army of 300 [they raised their voices, broke the pots, and gained a mighty victory]. David and Goliath [a shepherd boy swallowed his fear and by faith stepped in front of a giant and had the courage to voice his faith]. Abraham and Isaac. Shadrach, Meshach and Abednego. How about Paul in prison singing before the earthquake hit? How about the blind man who had to wash in the pool? Or the miracle of water into wine [it wasn't until it was poured out – that the folks at the wedding discovered its greatness]. There is power in discovery.

So today, I want to challenge you to embrace this truth - Learn something new! Study a brochure. Take a video class. Add a new word tract to your arsenal. Pump some life into your presentation. Get the customer involved more. Do some research on your product so you can relay that to your buyer. Stop doing it the same way every time because that is what you have always done.

Do a small act of obedience and then sit back and watch for the miracle. Who knows, perhaps you will surprise yourself. You just might learn that there is power in discovery. And that my friends, is one of the greatest strengths of sales. Or even in life in general. Remember, you are an inspired salesperson.

IV.   The Hippo Pit

"Commit your works to the LORD;
And your plans will be established." [Prov. 16:3 NIV]

Recently, I had the pleasure of attending the wedding of my granddaughter. The event was held at the zoo in a major city in the Midwest. The specific venue that the bride and groom had picked was a rustic lodge set back into the trees, a good hike from the entrance. As I parked, an attendant met me to give me directions on which path to follow, so that I wouldn't be late for the ceremony. Because it was early evening, I had no trouble following her advice. I walked a ways and as I came around a bend, I heard the rush of a fountain, and saw this beautiful place towering above me.

After the ceremony, [my granddaughter was so beautiful in her gown, by the way], the evening had turned to night, and the lighted pathway I had walked down before was now dark. [Apparently, the folks at the zoo had forgotten that there was a wedding going on, and accidently turned off most of the lights]. Determined to make my way back to the car, I set out by myself on foot. Without a phone [it was dead], or a flashlight, I followed the path I thought I was supposed to be on and ended up walking farther into the Zoo. Darker and darker into the jungle I walked. And the more ominous my path grew, the more nervous I became. Jungle sounds filled my ears [I heard a tiger growl behind me]. Now, instead of stopping and turning around, I kept walking, thinking that surely the exit was in front of me somewhere. I just knew that if I kept putting one foot in front of the other, I would eventually reach my car.

But unfortunately, that did not happen. Now, don't laugh. I actually had thoughts of the local news anchors coming out the next day, reporting on the disappearance of a man last seen leaving a wedding. The only evidence of his existence was a size 10.5 shoe left outside the gorilla entrance. No joke, I walked by the bird sanctuary, down toward the hippos, and even by the alligator pit twice.

It strikes me that a lot of new people who want to work in sales are the same way I was that night. They set out with the best of intentions, but end up getting lost. The darkness of the unknown envelopes them like the darkness of a jungle. And before they can find their way out, bad things happen. A manager loses confidence in them. A co-worker steals a deal. A customer gets mad and upset, all because the new trainee made a mistake and walked down the wrong path.

As a new salesperson, if you wander without a known path or a map, you will lose. In sales, there must be a process leading to the point of sale. Inspired salespeople must know where they are headed, and they must have a plan to get there. Without it, all that happens is a lot of confusion. Now to be honest, a sale can be made by someone without a plan. Occasionally, that can happen. As the old saying goes, "even a blind squirrel can find a nut every now and then". But to be inspired and successful in selling, it isn't just enough to bumble your way across the finish line. Inspired sellers want to sell everyone, and to do that, must have a process.

What is your sales process? In the sales business this is often called a, *the road to the sale*. It is basically the plan that the company wants you to follow, so that you can maximize your efforts with every single customer. It generally starts with greeting the customer and leads to discovering needs and wants, presenting a product with a demonstration possibly, closing, and then doing some sort of delivery, thank you and follow up. The dealership I worked for had 10 basic principles, but some companies have 6, 8 or even 12.

What is your company's *road to the sale?*

I am constantly amazed at the number of sales professionals who have no idea. Throw a pop quiz at the staff in a morning sales meeting, and most of them couldn't tell you the company's process at all. For a variety of reasons, either they have never been shown or trained on the steps to the sale or they were too lazy to learn it.

God sees value in establishing a plan. The Bible states, *"Commit your works to the LORD; And your plans will be established.* [Prov. 16:3 NASB]. *"Without consultation, plans are frustrated, but with many counselors they succeed."* [Prov. 15:22 NASB] or one of my favorite verses – *"For I know the plans that I have for you"*, declares the LORD, *"plans for welfare and not for calamity to give you a future and a hope."* [Jer. 29:11 NASB].

Even Jesus saw the value of a process. In one of his sermons, he talked about a man who built his house on the rocks, rather than the shifting sand. He weighed his options carefully. He counted the costs. He watched others build. And after careful consideration, the man determined that the best ground to build on was the solid earth of a rock and not the quicksand so many others had tried before.

A plan helps you prepare. A plan keeps the salesperson focused on the task at hand. A plan can lead to victory. That's why every sports team has a playbook and they practice that playbook constantly. They have meetings where they train on it. They memorize every play in the playbook in detail. Every successful company also has a process and they are committed to following it.

To be sure, in sales, customers do not always follow our scripts. The fact is that every customer is a unique person with different needs, wants and perceptions. But as hard as it may be to stay on track, great salespeople don't deviate from the road to the sale very often. They might take a side trip every now and then, but they always find a way back to the well-worn path. The road to the sale is their center. It is the ground of their being.

Think of it this way. Chances are you have used the GPS Map app on your phone. Ever driven to a new place and listened to Siri lead you to where you needed to go? "Your destination is on the right in 400 feet" it might say. How about when it screams at you constantly, *recalculating* when you take a turn it doesn't like? Without a road map, getting to a destination is always much more difficult.

So today, you have two assignments. First, write down the road map. Get the process to the sale firmly entrenched in your mind and determine to follow it. If you don't know what it is, ask your boss, your human resources director, your training manager, or even someone who has been at your company a while. Become the student. Study the map. Learn it. Remember you are an inspired salesperson.

The second assignment is a little more time consuming. You have to use the map daily. Let it flow from the head to the heart. It isn't enough just to know the directions if you don't follow them. When you follow the directions, finding the destination is so much easier. The truth is to be studious of the process and the principle behind that truth is to use the road map or end up being lost in the darkness every day! Just ask me, I'm still trying to find my way out of the jungle.

Was that a hippo I just heard?

*"We fail to investigate or perform
a customer needs analysis, and in our
hurry we 'serve' up the wrong thing."*

V. What Your Customer Wants

"But one thing is needed…" [Luke 10:41 NIV]

One of the best pieces of advice I ever received in the sales business was to slow down when I was in front of a guest. It's hard to do. Most of the time, our human nature as sales people tends to kick in when we are in the process of selling. The adrenalin is pumping. Excitement oozes from our pores. Our mouths salivate and are moving a mile a minute. Our mind tells us that there is an opportunity for a sale right there in front of us, and we don't ever want to miss the chance. We plow ahead toward the purchase, never realizing that we are missing a crucial aspect of great sales work; getting to know exactly what our customer needs and wants.

Ever returned an item because after you got it home, you discovered it wasn't' really what you thought it would be? We had that happen the other day at the place I work at. An elderly couple bought a vehicle and after 3 days of driving it, they brought it back. "We don't like it." I heard them say. Apparently, the salesperson had been in such a rush to make the sale, that he "stuffed" these folks into a car that didn't fit their needs. This couple just wanted was a car with basic features. They had told him that they were looking for a car that would get them from point A to point B, but the salesperson sold them one with all the bells and whistles. [Bigger commission, I suspect]. The technology in the car was too hard for them to understand. They couldn't even read the instrument panel. And what made matters worse is that they hated driving it, because they didn't feel safe in it.

There is only one way to determine what a customer needs, and that is to ask. Question asking is form of caring. It shows that you are more interested in the client's needs and wants than in lining your own wallet. When you slow down long enough to have a frank discussion about your guest's life experiences and expectations, you go a long way to building trust. The sale becomes more relationship based than product centered. And that's a good thing.

It strikes me that Jesus was the same way. If you read the gospels carefully, you notice that Jesus was never in a hurry. He wasn't so enamored with his power that he rushed through a miracle. He took his time, building relationships with his disciples and with the people His ministry impacted. When he preached, he told stories. Stories always take time.

Think about the day Jesus went to eat with Martha and Mary. It illustrates this principle perfectly. Remember how Jesus went to their house, and Martha was scurrying about the home, doing this and that. She was preparing the meal. Cleaning up the place. Serving the guests. Setting the table. It was a big task, trying to get food hot and ready for what was likely a couple of dozen guests. And in her hustle and bustle, Martha told Jesus to tell Mary [her younger sister] to get up and help. Where was Mary? She was simply sitting at the feet of Jesus, listening to his teaching, and hanging on his every word.

You can just hear Martha's indignation: "But Martha was distracted with much serving, and she approached Him and said, "Lord, do You not care that my sister has left me to serve alone? *"Therefore, tell her to help me"* [Luke 10:40 NIV].

Martha was so intent on the process of serving that she wanted Jesus to recognize the great effort she was making. And she also wanted Jesus to make others notice, too. In Martha's mind, it was all about her efforts. She wanted to be the center of attention. Her ego needed to be satisfied first.

I love how Jesus responds. Jesus looks at Martha and says, *"Martha, Martha, you are worried and troubled about many things".* *"But one thing is needed, and Mary has chosen that good part, which will not be taken away from her."* [Luke 10:41-42 NIV]

Take a moment to zero in on the first part of verse 41. Jesus said, *"One thing is needed…"* What was that one thing? In short, just to slow down and focus on the Person in front of you. Jesus wanted Martha to let lunch go. The dinner could wait. The menial task of serving could be put off for a bit. Even though, everyone's stomachs might have been hungry, there was a deeper hunger that needed to be fed.

Sometimes we salespeople are a lot like Martha. We are so focused on the process of making the sale that we scurry around trying to get this done and that done. We forget that inspired selling is born out of the relationship we have with the person right in front of us. We fail to ask the right questions. We fail to get information that can save everyone time and energy. We fail to investigate or perform a customer needs analysis, and in our hurry we *serve* up the wrong thing.

Most customers make a buying decision because they liked and trusted their sales person. So today, I want to challenge you not to be in such a hurry. Slow down when you are in front of a guest. Sit at their feet awhile. Get to know them. Build some rapport. Chat with them up. Ask about their kids, or their family, or their line of work. You could even inquire about what they are going to use the product they are considering for. And then, listen to their answers, take some notes if you need to and repeat things back to make sure you heard correctly.

To be an inspired salesperson, you must also be an inspired listener. The truth is to build rapport while you investigate the customer's needs. Remember, you are the inspired salesperson. You are the one who has such a good understanding of your customer, that you know exactly what they need and why. Be that person.

All though the Bible does not tells us, I would like to think that Martha set down the dishes, untied her apron, and took her seat right near her sister. Maybe it's time for you and me to do the same with the Person right in front of us.

VI.   You Gotta Sow to Grow

"He taught them many things by parables, and in his teaching said: 3
"Listen! A farmer went out to sow his seed..." [Mark 4:2-3 NIV]

Several years ago, while serving as the pastor of a rural church, I got a lesson in planting seeds. My sweet congregation wanted to be nice, so every Sunday for weeks; people kept giving me tomato plants. I didn't want to offend anyone, so I gladly accepted the gifts and took them home. Into the garden, they went. I planted fifty-one tomato plants that year. And every one of them produced a ton of tomatoes. In fact, we had so many tomatoes ripening on the vine that we couldn't pick them fast enough. We were swimming in the red stuff. We canned them into every kind of thing imaginable; pizza sauce, stewed tomatoes, spaghetti sauce, salsa, hot sauce and any other tomato recipe we could dream up.

Now when I received those seedlings, I had no idea if they would produce. In fact, before I could enjoy a nice BLT, I had to do a lot of work just preparing to plant. I pounded stakes and measured out where I wanted my garden. I loosened the dirt with a tiller. I convinced the dairy farmer down the road to dump a load of cow manure on the ground, which I then shoveled and raked all over the soil. I mixed the dung and the dirt with a tiller again. Then on my hands and knees, I made a hole, centered the plant down, covered it back up, and watered the heck out of them. And they grew. And they grew. And they grew some more.

Every inspired seller knows the value of planting seeds. The effective sales consultant realizes that each interaction he or she has is either a "present-day" sale or could be a potential one. *Remember most people buy because the like and trust the salesperson – which means that a good impression made today, might just win the sale tomorrow.*

Jesus knew the value of sowing. In one of his parables, Jesus tells of a farmer who goes out to the fields to spread his seed. He throws it out onto all kinds of different soil - some good dirt, some rocky, and some shallow ground. Now, as the farmer is working, he does not know how well the ground will produce. In fact, his hope is that every one of those tiny seeds will produce a hundred-fold. He looks forward to the harvest. There is great hope for the future when his barn is full and his family fed. But today, in this moment, the farmer has only one job to do – sow the seeds. The seeds must grow where it is scattered.

Take a moment to reflect on the story.

"As he was scattering the seeds, some fell along the path, and the birds came and ate it up. Some fell on rocky places, where it did not have much soil. It sprang up quickly because the soil was shallow. But, when the sun came up, the plants were scorched, and they withered because they had no root. Other seeds fell among thorns, which grew up and choked the plants. Still other seeds fell on good soil, where it produced a crop—a hundred, sixty or thirty times what was sown. Whoever has ears, let them hear." [Matt. 13:3-9 NIV]

In the parable, Jesus equates the seed to the Word of God, but in our example – think of the seed as information. Someone must be willing to take the seed [information] and with effort and energy [to the absolute best of their ability] spread it out where it can grow and produce. That's your job as an inspired salesperson. To take what you have learned about your product and to toss it out anywhere and everywhere you can.

I work with a friend who does this very well. He sows seeds [networks] all the time. I mean, all the time. He is a master of the video camera; shooting helpful videos on equipment, products and services. He has his own You-Tube channel where he promotes himself and his product. He is a *"master of social media"* and has gained a ton of followers. He is a member of civic organizations, attends chamber of commerce functions, and passes his card out to every person he meets. He is never ashamed to be a salesperson, in fact, he is quite proud of it. My friend will tell anyone who is willing to give him a few seconds, just how much he loves doing what he does. There is such an energy about him that it oozes from his pores. You can just sense it when you meet him. Over the years, he has watched the seeds he has scattered take root and produce. Most of the sales he makes today are from referrals and repeat customers, because of the hard work he has done in the past.

I think that the secret to my friend's success is that just like the farmer in the *Parable of the Sower*, he knows that not every soil will produce the same. While he tries to sell everyone, he is smart enough to know that some of his customers will be snatched away, like the seed on the path. Some customers will initially grow [be receptive to his words], but then other things in life happen, and the sale is lost. Some sales he loses to competitors [although not too often], like the thorns and weeds in the parable Jesus taught. Yet, no matter what the outcome – he knows that he has to keep spreading the word.

Just stop and think for a moment about the power of a single seed. An orange tree grows from a single seed. An oak tree begins from one acorn. A watermelon grows its vine from a single seed, and even tomatoes start by planting a seed in the soil. Did you realize that one simple seed has the power to produce a plant that in turn can create lots of abundant fruit and thousands more seeds which in turn can produce even more? Do the math. God has designed a means for us to sustain ourselves and others for years from the power of a single seed. It really is a shame that most of us throw these seeds away.

As the inspired salesperson, the truth is to be masterful enough to keep sowing the seed [networking and then following up with your customers]. A reminder phone call or text is a good way to keep your name in front of potential buyers. A card on a birthday, or special occasion or a simple post or like on their Facebook page can also go a long way. Maybe you need to create a presence on social media or get started taking a video with your phone. You just never know when a simple bit of information you plant will spring forth and produce a harvest. Today, I challenge you to sow some seed. Fertilize some old customers. Grow your business. Who knows after a bit, you might just be swimming in tomatoes.

VII.   The Value in The Daily

There is a right time for everything: A time to be born; A time to die;
A time to plant; A time to harvest; A time to kill; A time to heal;
A time to destroy; A time to rebuild. [Eccl. 3 NIV]

Y ou are an inspired salesperson, and for that, you should be
rewarded. Chances are when a sale is made in your
company, something almost magical happens. Maybe you
get a mark on the sales board next to your name. Your coworkers
applaud and cluck their tongues. The manager smiles and pats you
on the back, maybe even announces your name over the intercom.
Sell enough and you get a bonus! Close enough customers and you
can attend the convention in Vegas. Every organization finds ways
to reward and recognize its top performers, whether it is with a
plaque or a trophy or some other kind of perk.

We celebrate success and we should. The truth is that selling
is nothing if nothing is sold. Without results, it doesn't matter how

many clients are called or how great the salesperson's knowledge is. If he or she cannot deliver the goods, then the company makes no money, and the salesperson ends up unemployed. Or to make matters worse, a good person gets frustrated at the lack of success, which can lead to some very nasty heart issues [i.e. low self-esteem, bitterness, resentment – just to name a few].

Yet, as important as making the sale is, there is a lot more that goes into a deal than just the glory of pushing a set of wheels across the curb. Stop and think about the groundwork that needs to be laid for a sale to take place. A contact with a client must be made. The buyer must express some sort of interest. A salesperson must learn their product and be able to communicate the value of that item. Numbers must be agreed upon. Contracts printed and signed. Delivery of the product must align with a client's expectations. Follow up must be made. There are a hundred different mundane and ordinary tasks that almost always precede a sale. While moving another piece of inventory can be a glorious moment of accomplishment and inspiration, most of the time it is the result of a lot of effort. The excitement and adrenaline rush that comes with the "high" of closing the deal is just a small part of the process of selling.

I think at times it is easy to get so caught up in the hype of making the sale that we forget the value of consistency. The value of doing the work.

Too many companies trumpet the success and the rush of that final moment, without helping new employees understand the daily activities that are needed to make things really happen. Too many managers sell the sweetness of the victory, while holding back talking about all hard effort needed, because they do not want to overload or scare off the raw, fresh talent in front of them.

Don't get me wrong – sales can be a great profession. You can make a bunch of money in sales and earn a very good living.

It is just that inspired sellers know that the emotional high of a sale is temporary, and fleeting. Most of the time sales happen because of great effort and determination.

The Apostle Paul knew the value of doing the daily. Just think about what he wrote to the church in Philippians 3:12-14, *"No, dear brothers, I am still not all I should be, but I am bringing all my energies to bear on this one thing: Forgetting the past and looking forward to what lies ahead, I strain to reach the end of the race and receive the prize for which God is calling us up to heaven because of what Christ Jesus did for us."* [TLB]

Paul is saying that the end goal of reaching the prize is glorious, and that it is worth focusing on. But don't miss the fact that he knew that there was a lot of work that had to happen before claiming the prize. Words like bringing all my energies, and straining, forgetting what lies behind, show that Paul was pressing on daily. Moment by moment. Just think of how many miles Paul walked to minister to the various churches under his ministry. Think of the daily steps he had to take. The storms he had to endure. The cold and bitter nights. The prisons. In fact, he writes about that in the letter to the Corinthians –

"I have traveled many weary miles and have been often in great danger from flooded rivers and from robbers and from my own people, the Jews, as well as from the hands of the Gentiles. I have faced grave dangers from mobs in the cities and from death in the deserts and in the stormy seas and from men who claim to be brothers in Christ but are not. 27 I have lived with weariness and pain and sleepless nights. Often I have been hungry and thirsty and have gone without food; often I have shivered with cold, without enough clothing to keep me warm." [I Corinthians 11:26-28 TLB]

How does one develop a grit to persevere and keep going no matter what? You realize that every journey is made of steps. You embrace the daily mundane tasks that help build a foundation for future sales. When the manager asks you to make phone calls to clients, make them. When there are texts to be sent, send them.

When there are business cards to hand out, hand them out. Swallow your fear and get to networking. Don't find ways to get around the daily tasks your company wants you to do. In short, you must become a good student of time. Remember you are an inspired salesperson.

Here's the truth for the day – *Be mindful of your time.*

Perhaps today you and I need to be reminded of the value of the daily. The truth is to be good in sales requires a strong work ethic most of the time. When we sit down in front of our computers, let's remember that there are always things to be done. Ordinary things. Daily steps. Phone calls to make. Quota sheets to fill out. Reports to generate. Lessons to learn. We must slosh through the sloppy waters of the daily and the demanding in order to bask in the sunshine of the future sale. Be an inspired seller today. Learn to live and value the daily things.

"Learn to do common things uncommonly well; we must always keep in mind that anything that helps fill the dinner pail is valuable." - George Washington Carver

VIII.   The Plaques on The Wall

*"It is better to heed the rebuke of a wise person
than to listen to the song of fools."* – [Eccl. 7:5 NIV]

We hired a new salesperson the other day. When I walked into his office, I noticed that he had all kinds of plaques and awards from his previous jobs slathered all over the office. Trophy after trophy lined the shelves. *Top sales. Salesperson of the Year. Most units in a Quarter. Gross Profit awards.* There was barely enough room on his desk for a phone and computer. When I remarked about his choice of interior decorator, his feathers got ruffled a bit. He proceeded to tell me about how hard he had worked and the wonderful a job he had done to earn each accolade. You could tell that there was a lot of pride connected with those relics. After his tongue paused to take a breath, I reminded him that he still had to prove his worth to our company. I hoped that he would see his new career with us to grow and flourish and add to his collection.

He lasted two weeks.

Ever noticed how you can give a salesperson a little success and suddenly, they think they are God's gift to the selling universe? I have watched many consultants fall flat on their faces, because they didn't know how to keep their ego in check. Now, I admit that it is nice to get recognized for our achievements. If the boss gives you a plaque to hang on your wall, take it graciously, thank him or her and display it. When your peers applaud because you finished at the top of the leader board, you should enjoy the moment. There is no question that if you work hard, and the praises come, you ought to be recognized for the effort. But the truth is none of the awards really matters that much.

Keeping a sense of humility is an awfully hard thing to do in sales. I know that most of us who are good consultants are generally out-going, energetic, and high-functioning performers with sizeable egos. [I include myself in this assessment, by the way]. We feed on the praises of others. We love to bask in the glory of the spotlight. We take pride in getting great reviews online for the entire world to see. Most of us slobber over the applause of clients and company like a starving man drools in front of an all you can eat buffet. We crave the attention.

But the scripture above gives us a secret to keeping the swagger in check. Learn to accept praise and criticism constructively. When we surround ourselves with mentors and teammates who are wise, they can be a buffer against the pride that goes before the fall. The truth is that not every compliment should be internalized. Not every critique should be taken personally. In both instances, the words should be weighed as a path to deeper understanding and improvement. Use the kind words and the rebukes to make yourself better.

Just pause and think about the number of instances in the Bible where God encourages a person to heed wise counsel. From the opening pages of the book of Genesis, where God is admonishing Adam to listen to His Words;

"But the Lord God gave the man this warning: You may eat any fruit in the garden except fruit from the Tree of Conscience—for its fruit will open

your eyes to make you aware of right and wrong, good and bad. If you eat its fruit, you will be doomed to die." [Genesis 2:16-17 TLB]

To the closing pages of the book of Revelation, where the Apostle John writes –

"I, Jesus, have sent my angel to you to tell the churches all these things. I am both David's Root and his Descendant. I am the bright Morning Star." "The Spirit and the bride say, 'Come.' Let each one who hears them say the same, 'Come.' Let the thirsty one come—anyone who wants to; let him come and drink the Water of Life without charge." [Rev. 22:16-17 TLB]

Again, and again, God encourages those who need to hear to listen.

"Listen now to my voice; I will give you counsel, and God will be with you." [Exodus 18:19 NKJV]

"For they are a nation void of counsel, Nor is there any understanding in them." [Deut.32:28 NKJV]

"A wise man will hear and increase learning, And a man of understanding will attain wise counsel." [Prov.1:5 NKJV]

"But whoever listens to me will dwell safely, And will be secure, without fear of evil" [Prov. 1:33 NKJV]

"The ear that hears the rebukes of life will abide among the wise." [Prov. 15:31 NKJV]

"Incline your ear, and come to Me. Hear, and your soul shall live." [Is 55:3 NKJV]

"Whoever has ears to hear, let him hear…" [Luke 8:8 NKJV]

The Old Testament is filled with examples of how God sent prophet after prophet to help the nation of Israel turn back to him. *"I have also sent to you all My servants the prophets, rising up early and sending them,…but you have not inclined your ear to me."* [Jer. 35:15 NKJV] Anyway, you get the point. Listening to counsel and criticism is part of the secret to being successful in sales. The trouble is most of us are unwilling to heed the counsel of our superiors. We like the way we are. We see no reason to change. We think that we know better than the manager how to close the customer. We forget to trust the boss who has been in the business for twenty years, and just might know better how to do things than we do.

Let's face it – change is hard. And if you have had any success in sales, changing habits is much, much harder. I cannot tell you how many salespersons that have become so entrenched in the way that they approach a sale, that they lose sight of everything. So, when your boss tries to "load your lips" [telling you what to say to the customer] – nod your head and do it. Be obedient. Heed the wisdom of those who have traveled down the road to the sale before you.

Now, I am not suggesting that you tell the customer anything that is not true or trustworthy. [And if your boss asks you to lie or mislead any client, you should tell them you are uncomfortable doing so]. What I am referring to is how a young salesperson can get into trouble quickly, if they do not watch what they say. I have seen salespeople who have made promises or agreed to fix things, [only to find out later that they cannot deliver], and the scenario never ends well. When in doubt, ask. Be clear with your boss. Make sure you understand exactly what and how and when you should say what they want you to say.

And one more thing – just because you have a few plaques on the wall, does not entitle you to act any way you want. None of us is indispensable.

Remember, you are an "inspired" salesperson.

The truth is *"Don't get cocky"*. Learn the art of controlling your ego and you will live long in the sales business. In fact, you might make it past two weeks.

"Be careful. The junk that fills our minds can get away from us, and the ego that most sales consultants have keeps them from recognizing when it does."

IX.   U-Hauls Don't Lie

"Finally, brothers and sisters, whatever is true, whatever is noble, whatever is right, whatever is pure, whatever is lovely, whatever is admirable—if anything is excellent or praiseworthy—think about such things." [Phil 4:8 NIV]

I hate moving. Maybe you can relate. On more than one occasion, I have boxed up my family's stuff, and loaded all of our possessions onto a rental truck, so that we could make the trek to a new home. It's always a major hassle. Packing each box. Taping each box. Hauling each box. Arranging each box onto the back of a truck. Tying it all down, and then driving for hours in an old U-Haul bouncing up and down until my teeth rattle. Every time I go through this, I swear that I am never going to move again ever.

It isn't the moving or the renting of the U-Haul that bothers me. It's the sheer volume of unnecessary stuff I am faced with packing. It only takes one look at the junk that accumulates in my

49

garage to convince me that this going to be the last move I ever do. I vow that never again will I amass so much "stuff". Never again will I wait to clean out closets or empty drawers. I tell myself that from this point I will do a much better job of purging the things that clutter up my existence.

It occurs to me that there is a lot of worthless clutter that piles up in our sales brains, too. If we are not careful, a mountain of bad habits, shortcuts, and misconceptions can start filling our thoughts like the crap that accumulates in the garage. You might have watched a co-worker do something expedient that you knew was a bit shady and get away it. So, you adopted it. You might have been listening to the mediocre sales folks in the "huddle" complain. So, you internalized it. You might have listened to your own "press" and now, you are losing your edge.

Be careful. The junk that fills our minds can get away from us, and the ego that most sales consultants have keeps them from recognizing when it does.

The Bible reminds us again and again of how important it is to take a hard look at what needs to go and what needs to stay in our lives.

"Therefore, rid yourselves of all malice and all deceit, hypocrisy, envy, and slander of every kind..." [I Peter 2 NIV]

"But if a wicked person turns away from all the sins they have committed and keeps all my decrees and does what is just and right, that person will surely live; they will not die..." [Ezekiel 18:21 NIV]

"But unless you repent, you too will all perish." [Luke 13:3 NIV]

"Amend your lives therefore, and turn, that your sins may be put away, when the time of refreshing shall come from the presence of the Lord." [Acts 3:19 GNV]

Okay. I'll stop preaching. [I'm not thumping the pulpit at anyone else as much as I am trying to remind myself of the value of purging the manure that accumulates in my own heart and head].

The one thing about the junk in my garage is that I never really saw it. I was so busy dealing with the "daily grind of everyday life" that the trash in my garage just kept piling up. When I didn't know where to put something, out into the garage or into the junk closet it went. Shut the door and forget about it. Out of sight and out of mind was my mode of operandi. Like the old comedy sketch where the unsuspecting friend opens a closet to put away a coat and gets buried in a mountain of debris falling around him. If you wait to clean out your junk, the task of managing and clearing it can sometimes be too much. You become a hoarder of habits.

Inspired sellers are constantly working on keeping the clutter down. They don't let the non-professionals around them fill their minds with garbage. They are focused. Directed. Accountable. They grow themselves constantly; always learning new ways of presentation, better closes, or different word tracks to use. They read sales books and watch videos. They attend seminars. They find ways to be inspired. So, here's the challenge today. Do exactly what I did in my garage. Take a hard look at the stuff that has piled up, and start weeding through it. Keep the good sales principles, word tracks, and positive energies, but get rid of the junk. Believe me, you don't need it. You are better off without the dead weight. It just makes moving forward harder. Believe me, life is like a moving truck. It has a way of making you choose what needs to stay and what needs to go.

The U-Hauls don't lie.

"Most of what happens in sales involves communication. Whether it is a client interaction face to face, over the phone, via email, or something else — the choice of word plays a huge role in making the sale happen."

X.　It Starts When You Open Your Mouth

He who guards his mouth preserves his life, But he who opens wide his lips shall have destruction. [Prov. 13:3 NKJV]

The other day I made a mistake. I opened my mouth.

It was an innocent thing, to be honest. My intention was to be helpful to a friend by telling them something they needed to hear. They asked a question and I volunteered information. Not just a little, but a lot. Instead of answering the question simply, I turned the response into a full-blown lecture. [Words came spewing out of my mouth faster than a Kentucky Derby winner]. The result was not pretty. I soon discovered that my communication had left a trail of hurt feelings and bruised emotions behind them and I was oblivious to it all. I just kept on talking, when I should have just shut up.

Here is the truth. Most of what happens in sales involves communication. Whether it is a client interaction face to face, over the phone, via email, or something else – the choice of words plays a huge role in making the sale happen. Words are powerful. The right word at the right time in the right place said the right way can literally change the course of human history. Think about Patrick Henry yelling, *"Give me liberty or give me death."* Or Texans' cries of *"Remember the Alamo!"* or FDR who spoke about *"the only thing we have to fear is fear itself."* Even Martin Luther King's *"I have a dream"* speech inspired a movement and fostered great change. There are so many examples of how the spoken word has influenced people, created change, and even birthed nations that all the history books ever written could not contain them.

Even the Bible has a lot of examples of the power of speech. From the first pages of the book of Genesis, when God *spoke* and all of creation occurred, to Moses *calling* forth water from the rock, to Jesus summoning a dead man from the tomb – there is power in the spoken word. In fact, even salvation is dependent on the confession of a person's heart.

"If you confess with your mouth the Lord Jesus and believe in your heart that God has raised Him from the dead, you will be saved." [Rom 10:9 NKJV]

The trouble with most sales consultants is that they are not very articulate. They do a poor job of communicating to their customers. Instead of taking control of their words, they may speak with weakness or a lack of confidence. So often I see young sales consultants try to "wing" a sales presentation. These new sales professionals try to show the features of a product, but every other sentence is followed by dead space. They do not have a good enough grasp on their product or delivery to persuade anyone to do anything. They can appear fearful or shaky, or unprepared. Their words never add value to the product. Their vocabulary uses words that do not inspire a customer to purchase. Turning a "looker" into a "buyer" involves someone persuading another. Words matter.

What is it that lends words their power? What separates a word from just being a word to morphing into something more? Something that creates engagement and energy?

One of the most famous studies showed that words themselves account for about 7%, our tone accounts for 38%, and our body language makes up 55% of normal communication.

During the 1970's, researchers determined that a person often uses a speaker's body language to figure out truth – [true feelings, attitudes, and beliefs] about what someone says. [Albert Mehrabian's 7-38-55 Rule of Personal Communication].

Now before you jump on the bandwagon about how facial expressions, posture and eye contact are the essence of all communication, let me remind you that words are important. Without some skill in picking certain words over others, the inspired seller will not get very far. Almost every word carries with it a certain connation or visual image, and the effective salesperson knows this. How you describe things with the adjectives and phrases you use can mean the difference between making a sale or not.

Think about the words *payment* and *investment,* for example. Of these two words, which one sounds more positive? Making an investment in something or making a payment on an item? Customers hate "payments" but they are willing to make "investments". They hate monthly "obligations" but would prefer "options." Inspired sellers use words like simple, free, efficient, sleek, dynamic, convenient, stress-free, technological, tough, rugged, [just to name a few].

I call them value words. These are the words that carry with them more weight and tend to build up the value of the product in the customer's mind. There are words that will excite and enthrall. Phrases that provide comfort or piece of mind that will turn an ordinary person into a raving fan. Your job as a salesperson is to know which word or phrase will do that, so that you can maximize every opportunity you have.

Advertisers, writers and even some politicians have known the importance of using value words in delivering their content. Instead of tuning out the next commercial you hear, study it. Think about certain ads during a political campaign. Do you realize that someone somewhere sitting in some office pick every word you are exposed to? They wrote and rewrote and worked and reworked their "pitch" a hundred times over to create just the right effect on the ears that would be listening to it.

If you haven't taken a moment to examine your word choice, you should. Insert a new phrase. Make a list of descriptive words. Read a brochure and see how they present things. Simply, listen to a great sermon from a great preacher and see how they crafted their content. Learn from them. Ask yourself, why did they choose *that* particular word and insert it right there? Remember, you are an "inspired" salesperson.

Here is the truth here – learn the power of the RIGHT word. If the right word in the right place at the right time can change human history, surely it can help you make a sale.

XI.   Why More Than Value Matters

"You shall know the truth, and the truth shall set you free." [John 8:32]

The other day my wife asked me to pick up some laundry detergent on the way home from work. Being the dutiful husband that I am, I was happy to help. Without any hesitation, I swung into the store, found a great deal, bought it and headed home.

As I marched into our home, displaying the detergent like a caveman shows of his fresh kill, my wife met me at the door. In no uncertain terms she told me to carry my butt back to the store and get her the "right" laundry soap. I objected, [it was more of a whine], trying to convince her that the deal I'd found was better. Big mistake. She took the jug of detergent out of my hands and threw the full bottle into the garbage. "That," she exclaimed, "is what I think of your choice." I had no idea what to say. So back to the store I went. And to make matters worse, I was shocked to discover that the detergent my wife wanted was much more expensive than the stuff I had bought. Why would my wife pay such a high price for laundry soap? It couldn't clean *that* much better, could it?

I realized that my wife was willing to pay more for something because she perceived that it had the most value.

Have you ever thought about what it is that gives something value? Why would a consumer pay an astronomical price just to have a particular brand? What motivates a client to open their wallet just to buy their favorite cologne, pasta, clothing, or tickets to their favorite sporting event knowing full well that the cost of that item is through the roof?

The inspired salesperson knows that value of value.

The dictionary defines value as the, "relative worth, merit, or importance of something: the estimation of worth of an item." Clearly, my wife saw value in buying a certain kind of detergent. My autistic son knows the difference between the expensive and really cheesy mac and cheese as compared to the bargain brand. [He eats the regular stuff but inhales the cheesier noodles].

You probably have your own collection of items that you find worthy. You go to a great nail salon and are willing to pay more because it is your favorite. You buy a certain television set because the picture is better than other brands and you pay more for it. You drink a certain kind of craft beer, and it costs more. You drive a particular type of car or use a specific brand of tool, all because in your mind – the value exceeds the price.

Now to be honest, let's face facts. Some things are just better than other things. And the quality of an item can lend a lot to the idea of value. The workmanship of a piece of furniture might make the difference in the value of an item. How long an item lasts, or the speed it calculates, or the brightness of the picture, or even how an item makes us feel – all these qualities lead to increased worth. The inherent quality of an item can create value on its own. Sometimes even the price of an item lends to the perception of value.

But inspired salespeople know that is not always the case. Often, value has a lot more to do with the perceptions of the consumer than it has to do with quality or price. What I am talking about here is the word: *benefit*. The value the customer places on something rises in direct proportion to how much they believe they will benefit from having that thing in their lives.

For years, sales professionals have been teaching the difference between a feature and a benefit. A feature is basically what an item "is" as compared to the benefit ["what is does", or specifically how it applies to the customer's need]. A good presentation by a gifted salesperson never stops at just reciting the facts [features] of an item. It always transforms that fact and paints a picture to help the consumer understand why that feature is important [benefit]. This is "how" this "thing" will make the buyer's life "easier, better, safer, or more exciting" or whatever the case might be. I used to tell my students that until they had painted a visual picture in the mind of the person they were trying to persuade, nothing motivational happens. You can spew all the facts about a topic all day long, but if the client cannot relate to them, if the customer cannot see the benefit – he will never pay the price you are asking.

Think about the ministry of Jesus. He knew the best way to build value was primarily through two specific ways. First, He proved his power and love by *demonstration*. Every time Jesus healed the sick, fed the hungry, or raised the dead, He was showing God's compassion and power. As a result of these miracles, people were buying into his teachings in a way that amazed the religious zealots of the day. Just think about the crowds who followed Him, hanging on his every word. They saw the value of having a miracle worker like Jesus in their midst. You can create benefit in the mind of a consumer through demonstrations.

Think about the greatest verse in the Bible: John 3:16. If we were to break this verse down systematically, we could see the feature [God's Love], but also the benefit is made real through a specific demonstration. Take a closer look below.

"For God so loved the world [feature], *that He gave His one and only Son* [demonstration], *that whoever believes in Him should not perish, but have everlasting life"* [benefit]. [John 3:16 NIV]

There is value created because the feature [God's Love] was shown to us through a demonstration (Jesus) and the benefit is [not perishing but having everlasting life].

The other way Jesus created value was through teaching. He taught the masses about God. Sometimes it was through the speaking of basic truths like *"You shall know the truth and the truth will set you free."* [John 8:32 NIV] or *"Judge not, lest you be judged.* [Matt 7:1 NIV] *Notice the feature and the benefit.* At other times it was through parables or stories, [creating a mental picture in the mind of the listener to hammer a truth home]. For example, Then He said: *"A man had two sons....."* [the story of the prodigal son found in Luke 15:11-32 NIV]

Or the parable of the lost coin [Luke 15:8-10 NIV]:

"What woman, having ten silver coins, if she loses one coin, does not light a lamp, sweep the house, and search carefully until she finds it? And when she has found it, she calls her friends and neighbors together, saying, 'Rejoice with me, for I have found the piece which I lost!' Likewise, I say to you, there is joy in the presence of the angels of God over one sinner who repents." [NKJV]

So here is the point. An inspired salesperson [like you] knows that the best way to create value is to present the benefit. Perhaps today you need to work on developing this skill. Is your product presentation all facts and no fluff? Does it highlight a need without helping the listener know how your "product" meets that need? Does it give the customer a true mental picture of how you can save, help, aid, or cure? Without a benefit, no person will ever want to pay more for what you are offering. Without effectively showing the worth of an item, the only way to convince someone to make a buying decision is to cut the price to next to nothing.

So today, work on becoming articulate. Here is the simple truth - Presenting the *benefit* is much more powerful in helping someone buy into what you are saying than anything else you can do.

Just remember, sometimes even laundry soap can teach us stuff. Just saying.

"Think about the worst thing that might happen if you asked a customer for the sale."

XII.   If You Don't Ask, You Won't Sell

"You do not have because you do not ask…" [James 4:2]

My favorite book of the Bible is the book of James. This small New Testament book contains so many great truths that are so relevant for life and more specifically, a career in sales. For example, James tells us: *"So then,… let every man be swift to hear, slow to speak, slow to wrath…"* [James 1:19 NIV]

He also has lots to say about the power of the tongue. *"Even so the tongue is a little member and boasts great things. See how great a forest a little fire kindles."* [James 3:5]. Or how about – *"What does it profit, … if someone says he has faith but does not have works? Can faith save him?... For as the body without the spirit is dead, so faith without works is dead also."* [James 2:26 NIV] In other words, it is not enough to hope or even believe that something good can happen, if you are not willing to put what you believe into action.

One of the simplest statements in the book of James is this one: *"You do not have because you do not ask…"* [James 4:2 NKJV].

Did you realize that most of the time in the retail market, the transaction is generally not completed until the 5th time the sale is asked for? In other words, a lot of sales are missed because consultants fail to ask for the sale enough times. For whatever reason; fear, lack of training, or just plain laziness – sales people stop short. They let the customer walk away without capitalizing on the opportunity and pushing for the sale.

There are a ton of books written about how to effectively negotiate and close the sale. Many a sales guru has made a fortune teaching this or that word track, and a lot of them are very good. Yet, most of them miss this vital point. You just have to do it. You have to ask. Whether you use a *reduce to the ridiculous* or *a summary close* or a *takeaway close* – it doesn't matter as much as just working up the courage to open your mouth and ask. Look the customer in the eye and hit him with a close.

Ever failed to ask for something and ended up with egg on your face? I have. Years and years ago, my family and I went on vacation. We had loaded up the hatchback and decided to take a scenic route through a mountain pass. About twenty minutes up the winding switchback two lane road, [imagine a rocky mountain on one side and canyon-like ravine on the other] we ran into what can only be described as a cattle drive. Real life cowboys were driving about 500 head of cattle straight up the highway. As we inched our way up the highway, there were all sorts of emotions flowing in our car. My wife was snapping pictures out of the window, giggling every few seconds. My son thought it was better than Disneyland [the cowboys were riding horses]. My eldest daughter was crying because I was about to run over a baby calf, and I was fuming because our little car was being pushed around by a bunch of cows. The farther we got up the mountain, the higher the temperature gauge went on our car, and I could smell the clutch burning up. [We broke down about 75 miles later, in the middle of the badlands]. Unfortunately, part of the reason my family found itself in that predicament is that I was too stupid to ask for directions about the best route – instead I picked a road that was definitely harder than it should have been.

Think about the worst thing that might happen if you asked a customer for the sale. He might say, "No." And if he did, would that be so bad? There is a reason the customer is showing hesitation and giving off negative buying signals. Either they haven't been convinced of the value of the product, or they feel the price is too high, or dare I say it, they don't care for you all that much. [Most customers are too nice to come out and say they don't trust you to your face. They don't want to hurt your feelings].

Inspired sales people know that a negative answer to a closing statement is the doorway that almost every sale must walk through. The direct question only helps focus everyone's attention, and it allows for the true objection to rise to the surface. If the real reason for the shake of the head isn't somehow uncovered, then it cannot be dealt with and overcome. Just like it is impossible to fight an enemy you cannot see - it is also hard to deal with a hesitation that stays hidden. The truth is that once a sales consultant knows what they are up against, they can devote their energies into overcoming that specific objection and move on to closing the sale.

Perhaps today, you and I ought to take a cue from the book of James. Perhaps the reason we don't have more sales is because we have not asked. *You have not, because you do not ask.* The truth is to ask for the sale. And if the customer says, "No." find out why, and then ask again. And again. And again, if needed. Be persistent.

You might just find it'll keep you between the lines and the cows, so to speak.

"The inspired salesperson should speak truth when they sell, but they must also know the value of when to be quiet."

XIII.   The One Thing No One Can Refute

*"A time to tear, And a time to sew; A time to keep silence,
And a time to speak."* [Eccl. 3:7 NIV]

Sales is a *people* business. The sad reality of the matter is that our world is filled with sales consultants who don't seem to like people very much. Their body language and mannerisms exude a smug contempt for the very people who produce their paychecks. They mumble under their breath about the stupidity of clients, and make all kinds of excuses as to why they could not close the deal. Rather than learn from failure, these kinds of sales people tend to blame everyone else, instead of taking responsibility for their lack of skills.

Now I realize that customers can be difficult to work with. They can be rude, discourteous, and just downright mean when they do not get their way. I have seen more examples of lying and cheating by customers over the years than I care to mention. The truth is that no one sells everyone they meet, not even an "inspired" salesperson, because sometimes customers say they want to buy, but they plain don't. As the adage goes – *"you can't fix stupid"*.

Yet, clients aren't the only ones who can make inspired selling difficult. Sometimes, our teammates or our bosses can create barriers, too. Ever been in a sales meeting that was more a gripe session than a constructive meeting to address a problem? Ever had to listen to the malcontents and the naysayers rev up their engines, only to leave their fellow employees choking on the exhaust of their dissatisfaction? I've been around a few folks in the sales world whose rants and railings were so rancid they made a rabid dog look tame. One time a manager climbed up on his desk to remind us who was the king of the castle and we were nothing but starving peasants. Another time, a salesperson who disagreed with something that was said, walked to the center of the sales floor and screamed obscenities at customers and staff before he stormed out. The very first time I witnessed this kind of spit-drooling tirade, it scared me a lot. But over the years, I have learned to let idiots be idiots.

What's the secret to inspired selling when someone around you decides to be difficult? When the boss seems to resist every notion? What do you do when someone doesn't want to play "nice"?

The answer is simple.

Keep your mouth shut. The one thing no one can refute is silence.

The inspired salesperson should speak truth when they sell, but they must also know the value of when to be quiet. Even though a lot of what the sales process encompasses depends on good communication, silence plays a pivotal role. Sales isn't just about knowing how to persuade someone to the point of a buying decision, it is also about knowing when to stop talking. Eventually in every sale there comes a time when the pitch has been made, the facts have been laid out, and a decision is needed. The numbers have been presented, and now a client must choose one. A price has been negotiated and it is up to the buyer to pick up that pen and sign their name. It doesn't matter whether you are selling cars or vacuum cleaners, there comes a time when the salesperson should stop speaking and get the sale or keep pressuring the client and talk everyone out of it. [It takes a lot of wisdom and practice to know the difference].

The book of Ecclesiastes tells us that there is a *"A time to tear, And a time to sew; A time to keep silence, And a time to speak..."* [Eccl. 3:7 NKJV]

The Psalmist said, *"Keep your tongue from evil, And your lips from speaking deceit."* [Psalm 34:13 NKJV]

The writer of Proverbs put it this way – *"Death and life are in the power of the tongue, And those who love it will eat its fruit."* [Proverbs 18:21 NKJV]

Stop and think of the value of silence. Jesus understood this concept well. When being brutalized and beaten by the scribes and Pharisees, he did not open his mouth. When the crowds called for his blood, with shouts of *"Crucify Him, Crucify Him"* – he kept quiet. His meekness surprised Pilate. The Bible tells us that *"Pilate asked Him again, saying, 'Do you answer nothing? See how many things [they testify against You!' But Jesus still answered nothing, so that Pilate marveled."* [Mark 15:4-5 NKJV] The reason was because the die had been cast. God's plan to redeem humanity was unfolding exactly as it was supposed to. This was the point in human history where Jesus had done everything he should have to prove the value of who He was. There was no need for trying to continue to justify anything. In this case, silence was the better play.

69

Most sales consultants miss this great truth, because they cannot stand the silence. They hate the awkwardness of it. They talk over everyone. They have to be the loudest in the room or the one who has the last word. They are so enamored with their own selves that they try to wear the client out with all the stuff they know. Often, these sales *professionals* come off as condescending and arrogant because they have convinced themselves that they know better than their client exactly what is needed. I think Ben Franklin said it best, *"Better to hold your tongue and have others think you the fool, then open your mouth and remove all doubt."*

So today, watch your tongue. When things get silent during a negotiation, just breathe. It's okay that things are getting quiet. That might be a signal that the client is primed and ready to pull the trigger. Let the chips fall where they will. Be confident that you have done everything you were supposed to do to set up the sale.

Remember, you are an inspired salesperson. And an inspired salesperson knows when not to talk themselves out of a sale.

XIV.   Hero to Zero

When he came near the place where the road goes down the Mount of Olives, the whole crowd of disciples began joyfully to praise God in loud voices for all the miracles they had seen:

> *"Blessed is the king who comes in the name of the Lord!"… "Peace in heaven and glory in the highest!" …. As he approached Jerusalem and saw the city, he wept over it and said, "If you, even you, had only known on this day what would bring you peace — but now it is hidden from your eyes."* [Luke 19:37-38; 41- 42 NIV]

E very month it happens. If you are a salesperson, or work around sales folks, you know that each month we go from "hero to zero" in a heartbeat. One moment you are basking in the glorious praise of a great month. You made your quota, got a bonus check, won the accolades and admiration of

71

bosses and coworkers. And then, the first of the month rolls around and the sales board is wiped clean. The old numbers are forgotten. It is ancient history. The boss demands a new quota or goal be established, and you begin to work your tail off to produce the fantastic results you know you are capable of.

Sales is a very "what have you done for me lately" business. Your owner or boss will be the first to tell you that it doesn't matter how great you were yesterday, what matters is being great today. You can be the best salesperson in the world, but if you have an off month or quarter, you will certainly hear about it or worse be unemployed. The constant pressure and stress of having to make "the grade" keeps a lot of people from dipping their toes into the sales waters at all.

Stop and think for a moment about Jesus. He was probably the greatest communicator in all of human history. His words moved masses. His teachings and actions have been professed by countless generations for over two thousand years. He began a movement that literally turned the world upside down. Since His feet have touched the clay of this world, almost nothing has been the same. If anyone deserves "hero" status, it was [is] Jesus.

If you read the gospels closely, you will discover something interesting. Jesus went from hero to zero almost overnight. One moment the city of Jerusalem was singing his praises, yelling chants of "Hosanna" and the next the same people were cursing him and crying for his death. Hero to zero. The scriptures even tell us how Jesus reacted to that moment. On the day when He should have been basking in the glory of everyone's admiration, soaking up the praises of the people, the Bible says that He wept. Knowing what was about to happen, He cried out and shed tears over the city.

Inspired sellers know that the monthly [daily] agony they feel as the sales numbers are erased from the board is nothing to the pain Jesus felt. He knows what it means to go from greatness to nothing. He understands the fickleness of our world better than anyone. He knows that there is no loyalty by any consumer. If they think you aren't meeting their expectations, they will drop you faster than you can say the Lord's Prayer. He understands your disappointment when you want to bask in the limelight but can't because others will not allow it. If you lost a sale today, remember the day Jesus lost the love and respect of almost everyone He had ever ministered to.

So today, take some comfort in the fact that Jesus knows. He's been there. Don't fret about the numbers you made. Even though, that is ancient history to some, He sees your hard work. Instead of worrying about the attention you think you deserve, focus on the task in front of you. That's exactly what Jesus did. He set his mind to the business of dying on the cross for the sins of the world. Believe me, that was a much harder quota to fill than any sales number you or I are trying to achieve. Remember, you are an inspired salesperson. Inspired sellers forget what lies behind and press onto the high calling. If you don't think that is so, just ask Jesus.

"Wallow in the blackness of the night long enough, and the drive to succeed will flicker out like the flame of a dying candle."

XV.   The Absence of Light

"Even the darkness will not be dark to you; the night will shine like the day, for darkness is as light to you." [Psalm 139:12 NIV].

Every sales professional goes through tough times. There are moments when it seems as if the sales simply will not come. Every call we make ends badly. Every presentation we pitch falls on deaf ears. Every close we consider wraps up with a shake of the head, and a polite, "No, thank you" spilling from our client's lips. Despite our very best efforts, it seems as if no one wants to buy. And the longer the drought, the darker a salesperson's heart and mind can become. Wallow in the blackness of the night long enough, and the drive to succeed will flicker out like the flame of a dying candle.

What most sales consultants do during tough times is that they complain and whine. They offer excuses. They lament about the stupidity of customers, bosses or co-workers. They offer all kinds of reasons why sales are down. If only the boss would spend more money. If only the dealership hadn't hired some many "new" "internet people". If only the government would stop fiddling with interest rates, then maybe something might change. *If only* becomes the mantra of the day, coupled with the "*I remember when*" of the glories gone by. Ever noticed that there is just something in the human heart that believes that if we grumble loud enough, the dessert will somehow become the land of promise?

In sales, about the only thing a negative attitude will get you is fired. Most managers do not have time to cater to an employee they view as a cancer. And if the supervisors are worth their weight at all, they will take steps to remove that contentious employee long before he or she damages the minds of others around him. In most retail fields, managers often make "snap" decisions on the worth of their employees. Sometimes even after just a few hours of work, it is clear to a boss that the new hire isn't going to cut it.

The children of Israel experienced this firsthand. They spent 40 years wandering through the wilderness, shuffling along in the sand of a barren wasteland. And these people, whom God had chosen as His own; griped, grumbled, and murmured every weary step of the way. They meandered around in the desert, never really learning the lessons God was trying to teach them. And what did all their complaining get them? Just the same stuff every day; the same food, the same water, the same pillar of cloud and fire [which was a blessing they couldn't see]. Nothing changed even though their bickering was loud enough to rattle the gates of heaven.

Need another example?

Consider the life of David. As a young man, he stood up to a giant. With faith, he led the nation of Israel and penned some of the most beautiful songs history will ever record [just read the book of Psalms, if you don't believe me]. At times, his faith seemed

76

invincible. He would declare his allegiance and the wonder of all that God was doing in him and through him.

> *"The law of the LORD is perfect,*
> *refreshing the soul.*
> *The statutes of the LORD are trustworthy,*
> *making wise the simple.*
> *The precepts of the LORD are right,*
> *giving joy to the heart.*
> *The commands of the LORD are radiant,*
> *giving light to the eyes.*
> *The fear of the LORD is pure,*
> *enduring forever.*
> *The decrees of the LORD are firm,*
> *and all of them are righteous.*
> *They are more precious than gold,*
> *than much pure gold;*
> *they are sweeter than honey,*
> *than honey from the honeycomb."*
> [Ps. 19:8-10 NIV].

These are the words of a man in a deep relationship with God, who loves to feast on God's Word.

But at other times in his life, David struggled to find God's presence.

For example – In Psalms 42:1-4 – he cries out to God:
> *"As the deer pants for streams of water,*
> *so my soul pants for you, my God.*
> *My soul thirsts for God, for the living God.*
> *When can I go and meet with God?*
> *My tears have been my food*
> *day and night,*
> *while people say to me all day long,*
> *"Where is your God?"*

77

From the perspective of the divine it is helpful to know that God sees us when we go through the crisis of despair. Even in the blackness of the longest night, God knows the struggles we have trying to find our way. He occupies the void. As the psalmist says, *"where can I go from your presence? Where can I flee from your Spirit? If I ascend into heaven, You are there; if I make my bed in [a]hell, behold, You are there."* [Psalm 139:7 NKJV] In other words, God is there, wherever you are. It does not matter whether we are standing on the mountaintop of success or wallowing in the valley of despair, God is there. Interestingly enough, if you "google" the word, darkness, the internet defines it as the absence of light. While that might be the way our world sees it, it is not the viewpoint of eternity. The absence of light does not mean the absence of the Heavenly Father.

So today, if you are struggling to keep your attitude up, take comfort in the One who knows where you are. To have success in sales we must live in the Presence of God through every moment. Trust Him to carry you forward. Use the dry places to refine yourself, work on your mindset, and improve your dependence on Him. You will get through it. And when you do, you will remember the journey through the darkness. Soon, you will bask in the sun of a new day. Not because of who you are, but because of who He has always been. Because of who He is. Because of who He will always be.

Remember, even the darkness is as light to Him.

XVI.   Lick the Bowl

*"God has delivered me from going down to the pit,
and I shall live to enjoy the light of life."* [Job 33:24 NIV]

Recently, I was walking down the aisle of a home improvement store looking at some clearance items, when one of those painted inspirational signs caught my eye. It said, *"Enjoy life, lick the bowl."* I couldn't help smiling. I thought about the days when I was growing up, how my mother would make brownies or a chocolate cake. As she was putting the pan in the oven, she would holler at my little sister and I to come into the kitchen. "Here." She would say, as she handed over the mixing bowl, "Enjoy." And the two of us would fight over who got to lick the bowl clean. That delicious batter was heaven to our taste buds. You can bet that each of us scraped that bowl spotless, devouring every tiny morsel of chocolate goodness we could get.

That sign held the secret to a happy life.

Yet there was a problem. As I picked it up, I noticed a couple of things. First, the item was marked down to next to nothing and tossed onto the clearance rack to be forgotten. A layer of dust and a few scratches and a dented corner told me that this little sign had seen its share of struggle over the months and years.

This is exactly how people are. Too often, we get so consumed by the scratches and dings of daily life, that we forget to enjoy the moments. When we stop enjoying life, the days and months and years speed by. Birthdays are missed. Warm smiles and hugs go undone. What should be said is left unsaid. We fail to remember that every minute that passes is a minute gone forever. In short, we place ourselves on the back of the clearance rack, hoping our existence will change, but knowing that it likely never will. Before long we forget why we were even created. Like the sign that had a glorious message to deliver, we left someone or something else determine our fate. We rot in the place where we do the least good.

There is a cure for this, you know. You have to do two things.

First, you just have to lick the bowl when life gives you a treat. Enjoy the little things like time spent with family. A good productive day at work. The smile of friend. Take time to go fishing. Breathe in some fresh air with a walk. Learn to love just being present. [Sales is a very "present" business. That is one of the reasons I love it and the people who persevere in it.]

Speaking of living in the present - during the last few months of the recent COVID-19 pandemic, God has certainly pumped the brakes on daily life. As most of the nation has been under stay at home orders, there was a new reality forced on us. We had to reconnect with the family. Mom's had to reinvent how to fill up the hours of the day, with meaningful moments. Teachers were forced to abandon the physical classroom and teach through video. Companies were forced to outsource or hold meeting via the Web. We all learned that just a simple Skype chat or a wave through a nursing home window could create the strongest of moments. So many families were forced to relearn how to live with each other in the same space at the same time. It was God's way of forcing a shift back to the importance of licking the bowl.

The second thing? Remembering that the best is yet to come.

You see, when my little sister and I fought over the morsels of chocolaty goodness, the remnants in the bowl were only a pre-taste of what we were about to enjoy later. As the smell of my mother's baking wafted through the air, I knew that in about an hour, I was going to dig into more chocolate awesomeness. I enjoyed the batter, but frankly, the brownies were so much better.

So today, I want you to enjoy your life. Just slow down. Make your work environment a fun place to be. Not just for yourself, but for others as well. Stop and experience the depth of love, the width of friendship, the height of great effort, and the breadth of God's plan for you. Pause from your daily routine long enough to remember that the person on the other side of the desk [or the kitchen table] is more than you first thought. See them for who they are – wonderful creations of our Heavenly Father.

Don't forget – the best is yet to come. You are not today what you will be tomorrow. Today is only a small *early taste* of the glory that God has for each of us. And one day, when He decides, we will be as He is. In the meantime, lick the bowl. In fact, I think I hear my mom calling me to the kitchen right now.

"But the reality is that it takes a great deal of work to pitch our tent where He is."

XVII.   Where You Dwell

"Splendor and majesty are before him; strength and joy are in his dwelling place.." [I Chronicles 16:27 NIV]

Several years ago, I took my family camping under the mountains of the Tetons. The particular campground that we stayed in was so popular that you had to make reservations months in advance just to be able to stay there. When we arrived, we were fortunate enough to get a camping site that looked like it was straight off a postcard.

We were at the edge of a crystal-clear lake with the forest all around, and the majesty of the mountains towering above us. As my family and I paused to take in beauty of God's creation, I remember standing there just breathing in the smell of the pine trees, watching the chip monks scurrying this way and that, reflecting on how glorious God's handiwork truly was.

I could have stayed in that moment. But I didn't.

If you have ever been in the mountains, you know that at night it gets cold, even in the summer months. So after a few moments of reflection, my family and I got to work, unloading all the stuff we had brought. The tents came out. The stakes were driven into the dirt. The ropes were tied; sleeping bags unrolled and the lanterns lit. My wife prepared the cook stove and started on dinner.

My son collected firewood, while my daughters supervised. Everyone in the family had a job to do. After a couple of hours, we were roasting hotdogs and making smores in front of a blazing, warm fire. Even more importantly, we were building memories. We were living out the daily under the cathedral of God.

And it was perfect.

The truth is we all live somewhere. I am not speaking about our place of residence or the home we call our own as much as the state of mind which occupies our thoughts. Let's face it, every day we can choose to pitch our tent in a place of grace, goodness, and love or in a place of bitterness, defeat, and anger.

It strikes me that the writer of the passage above had a similar thought. God is indeed filled with splendor and majesty. Strength and joy are where He dwells. His desire is that we live there, so that what is His is ours. We should live the daily surrounded by the Holy.

But the reality is that it takes a great deal of work to pitch our tent where He is. If we are not careful, the pressures of the day and frustrations brought on by difficult people can close in on us like the brisk night air of a mountain forest. If we are not willing to do the hard work of intentionally setting up camp, each moment choosing strength and joy over anger and hurt, we may find ourselves in the pitch black - freezing from the cold. Of course,

God is still there, even in the darkness but the beauty and the majesty of who He is are momentarily obscured from our view.

Ever since the Garden of Eden, mankind has been faced with the same choice. Adam and Eve could have chosen to dwell in the very presence of their Maker, but they let outside influences distract them. The children of Israel could have dwelt in the Promised Land and found the land flowing with milk and honey, but instead they chose to pitch their tents in the wilderness. Elijah could have trusted in the power of God's might, but instead hid in a cave.

King Herod could have bowed his knee in worship to the newborn King, but instead sent his troops to kill innocent children. Even Jesus wept over the city of Jerusalem, pleading with the crowds to gather under the shelter of his wing, but instead in short order, they cried for his blood. Judas Iscariot could have grown and flowered under the instruction of the Master, but instead sold him for thirty measly pieces of silver. Again, and again, we choose to live in the Presence of God or in the wasteland of indifference and darkness.

Where do you dwell? Where have you pitched your tent?

"Let the trees of the forest sing, let them sing for joy before the Lord." [I Chron. 16:33 NIV]

"The LORD is my strength and my shield; my heart trusts in him, and he helps me. My heart leaps for joy." [Ps 28:7 NIV]

"Led in with joy and gladness, they enter the palace of the king." [Ps. 45:15 NIV]

Today, make it a point to live in the place of joy. It is a strong place. Take just a moment to bask in the beauty of who God is. Then get to work.

Prepare the meal. Build the campfire. Unroll the sleeping bags. Pitch your tent. Do the work of the daily in the presence of the Holy and see if that doesn't fill the night air with laughter and warmth. Just like a night under the Tetons.

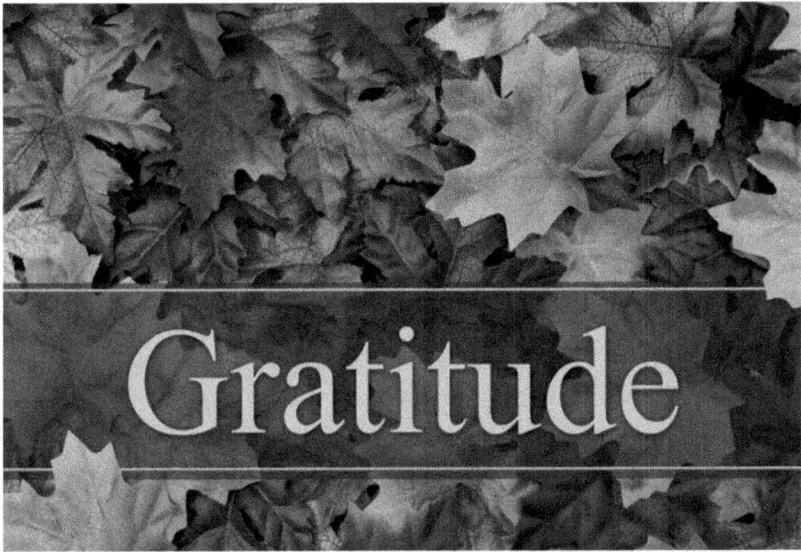

XVIII.   A Good Thing

"How abundant are the good things that you have stored up for those who fear you, that you bestow in the sight of all, on those who take refuge in you." [Psalms 31:19 NIV]

I have a special needs child who has a favorite line he likes to repeat. Any time he agrees with something, or likes what he hears, he says, "It's a good thing." Grill burgers? A good thing. Go shopping? A good thing. Play with the dog? A good thing. Watch Garfield and Friends? A good thing. Hear a song he likes on the radio? A good thing. Get a smile or a hug? A good thing. Help Dad in the yard? A good thing. You get the point. A thousand times a day, my autistic son reminds me of the importance of being grateful. Not just for the big things, but for everything.

I got to thinking about this a lot lately. I've heard preachers talk about having an attitude of gratitude in everything and part of me has always been skeptical about it. I mean, no one can be truly grateful in everything, can they? My usual thought when I hear a sermon about gratitude is on the order of - *"If only you had to live my life, you wouldn't be rejoicing 24 - 7."* I mean, with the daily pressures and frustrations that constantly bombard us, how is it possible to be thankful for anything and everything that comes our way?

And yet my son doesn't see it that way. His worldview is so simple. He continually reminds me and anyone who will listen that the world is filled with stuff that is good. Now, truth be told, he isn't perfect. Does he get frustrated by things? Sometimes. Does he get stubborn and not want to comply with a request his mother makes? Occasionally. Does he get sad about things happening in his life every now and then? Certainly. But he always comes back to where his universe is centered. The good things. From his lips comes the secret to true and lasting contentment.

There are lots of instances in the Bible where God reminds us to be mindful of all He has done for us. In fact, in the book of Deuteronomy, these are the words spoken to children of Israel.

"Now it shall come to pass, if you diligently obey the voice of the LORD your God, to observe carefully all His commandments which I command you today, that the LORD your God will set you high above all nations of the earth.

And all these blessings shall come upon you and overtake you, because you obey the voice of the LORD your God.

Blessed shall you be in the city and blessed shall you be in the country.

Blessed shall be the [a]fruit of your body, the produce of your ground and the increase of your herds, the increase of your cattle and the offspring of your flocks.

Blessed shall be your basket and your kneading bowl.

Blessed shall you be when you come in and blessed shall you be when you go out." [Deut. 28:1-6 NKJV]

Did you notice how often the word "blessed" is used? Again, and again, God tries to get the nation of Israel to understand that if they will only follow Him, their lives will be so much better. Their families will grow. Their herds will increase. The ground they toil will overflow with an abundant harvest. The daily activities that they perform [the basket and kneading bowl] will result in a surplus of food. No matter if they are waking up to start a new day or laying their head on their pillow at night, [blessed when you come in; blessed when you go out] abundant things will be there. And did you notice that the blessings don't just come to them, but literally "overtake" them. Like a tsunami of God's favor hitting the shore and sweeping everything they have along in the current.

Maybe that's what God is trying to say to us. Maybe it's not so much about rejoicing when our world is caving in around us, as it is, remembering our center. Remembering that no matter how awful life is, God is still there. The air we breathe is a good thing. The job we have - that is a good thing [better than being unemployed probably]. The family we go home to - a VERY good thing. The kiss of a grandchild - a good thing. The eyes to see a sunset. The smile of a friend. The encouraging word spoken our way. Our world is filled with so many good things that we scarcely take the time to notice. Every moment, God keeps showering down blessings, waiting for us to acknowledge them. But instead of answering these blessings, we put God on an indefinite hold like some boiler room call center.

So today, your task is to reflect on this - Rejoice in the good things God does for you every day. Take a moment to be thankful for each and every person you meet. Reflect on each interaction as an opportunity to build a relationship or renew a friendship. Remember you are the inspired salesperson. The psalmist had it right when he wrote, *"How abundant are the good things you have stored up...."* [Ps. 31:19 NIV]   Take a moment just to whisper a prayer of praise to your Maker for all the good stuff He bestows on you. Today, I am taking a page out of my son's life manual.   Today, I will rejoice in the "good things."   Will you?

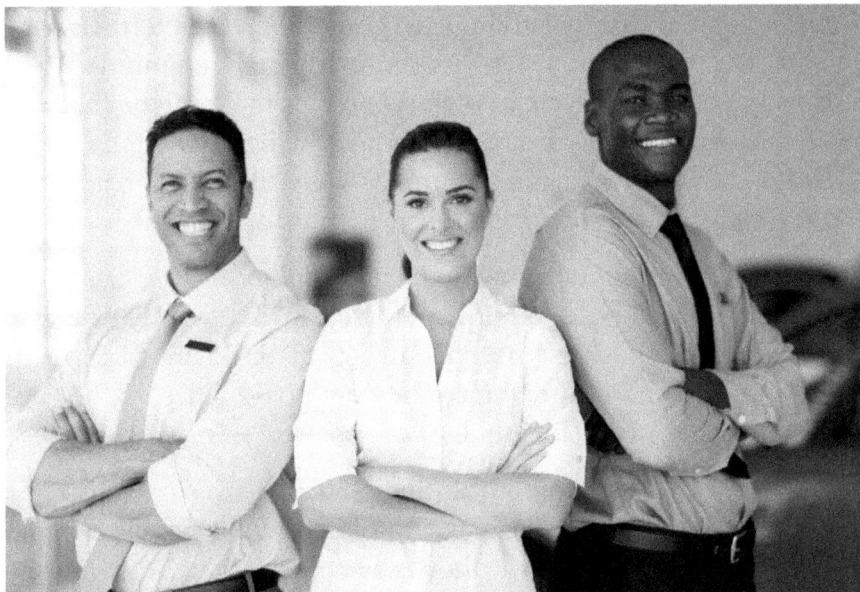

XIX.   THE POWER OF TEAMWORK

Therefore encourage one another and build each other up,
just as in fact you are doing. [I Thes. 5:11 NIV]

In 1519, the Spanish Conquistador, Herman Cortés stood on the beach of a new world and proclaimed it to be under the sovereignty of Spain. While the journey across the Atlantic had not been easy for him or the 500 men who had traveled with him, he believed that great things were ahead of them. This strange new world was completely uncharted and unconquered, and he had no doubt that it held wondrous riches. To be sure, the future was unknown, but his faith in the glory of Spain and in God's divine plan would drive him and his men forward to fulfill their destiny.

To ensure that his soldiers understood the gravity of this new mission, he gave the command that the 11 ships they had the skinny truth sailed on should be scuttled and then burned. His order insured that he and his men could not return to their former lives, and would now have to be completely committed to the cause of conquering the new world. As his men watched their only lifeline back to their families and homes being destroyed, I can only imagine that their hearts and minds were filled with fear of what they might face in the days and weeks ahead.

Throughout the ages, the phrase *Burn the Boats* has become the clarion call to commitment. Recently, I was listening to a motivational speaker who encouraged his listeners to leave their old lives behind and embrace the new possibilities of the future. *"If you want to change,"* he said, *"You gotta burn your boats."*

Yet, every time I hear that phrase, it gives me pause. Stop and think about what the average soldier must have been thinking as he watched his only way home being destroyed before his eyes. The fear and sadness of seeing that spectacle must have been enough to overwhelm him. Would he live or die in the days and weeks ahead? Would he ever see the gentle farm he had been raised on again? Would he hold the woman he loved? Kiss the face of his child?

Despite the fear, the men under Cortes' command went forward. Not one soldier deserted. Not one started a revolt to overthrow Cortes and rebuild the ships so that they could return. Were these hardened soldiers so committed and loyal to Cortes that they allowed him to do anything with their lives and futures? Perhaps. But I don't think so. Did the stories of gold and glory so fill their minds that it drove them through the thick tangle of brush, step by step by step? Maybe. Did the fear of being executed if they disobeyed their commander make them tow the line? Possibly. What was the motivation that made them hack their way through hundreds of miles of dense jungle, endure harsh conditions, and eventually conquer this new land?

If it had been me, I might have been tempted to walk away. In my mind's eye, I can see myself standing up for my rights. Demanding to be heard. I would have dropped my armor and told Cortes where he could go. I might have tried to enlist the help of a few loyal friends to see what we could do to *fix* the situation. There is no way I would have followed a lunatic, no matter how strong and devoted to the country he might have been.

And it would have been the wrong choice because likely, I would have died alone.

I'll tell you what I think was going on. Each soldier understood this fact: that they had a much better chance of surviving if they stayed together. They needed each other. They would have to depend not on their commander, but on each other. While they may have been a company of ordinary soldiers before the journey, Cortes' actions now insured that these men would become something more. They would become brothers, even family.

As managers and employees, we underestimate the power of inspiring teamwork all the time. What happens in most places is that bosses spend their days trying to direct the staff, [primarily by catching them doing things wrong and then trying to correct their mistakes]. Leaders preach the process and educate on the procedures. Supervisors remind and coach and caution. Owners thump their desks in judgment when the organization does not seem to perform as it should. Sometimes a company can have such a tunnel vision about the bottom line that it fails to foster any kind of a team atmosphere. And this lack of synergy can often lead to a culture of low morale that can cripple a company in the long run.

Now, don't get me wrong. Numbers are important. Profit is not a bad word. Inspired salespersons need to make all the money they can for their employer. But so is teamwork. Teamwork can help develop the kind of environment that makes making money fun and easy.

You have to hand it to Cortes. As crazy [or sensible] as it might have been to burn the boats, his actions inspired 500 men to move forward, while at the same time, bringing them together in a way that no words could. The real credit should go not to Cortes, but to the men who did an incredible job of inspiring each other. When the mud got thick and the rains came, they huddled together. When the snakes slithered around them, and the wild animals attacked, they watched each other's back. When the rations got low, they shared with each other. When there were cuts and broken bones and malaria fevered their comrades, they carried the bodies of the sick on their backs.

Inspired sellers know the value of helping others. They understand the power of teamwork. While they may burn some boats every now and then, they stand together with their fellow brothers in sales, even when everything around them may be going up in flames. So today, if you are a sales consultant, *help a brother up*. When you see one of your fellow soldiers become weak and need help, lift their spirits. Encourage. Affirm. Congratulate a success. Support each other. Carry a pack for a while. Don't expect anything in return. It's not about who owes who. Inspired sellers understand that every member of the team is valuable, no matter how weak they might be. And if you are a manager, please get your team together and give them a "thank you." Inspire. Don't just educate or correct, but spend some time energizing your team to be more than conquerors. Be the leader you were meant to be. Be the team member you need to be. And who knows, you might just change the course of human history. The men of Cortes did.

XX.   TRUTH TELLING

"Speak the truth in love." [Eph. 4:15 NIV]

When I was in the ministry, there was an old adage that someone once told me: *"Tell the truth and trust the people."* In short, it meant that whenever a mistake happened, the man in the pulpit should admit it, own it, and then trust that the decision of the congregation [and God] was for the best.

In some cases, even if that meant having to find a new church or a new line of work altogether.

We live in a world of false truths. Lies spill from the lips of politicians and entertainers like tap water from a faucet. From governmental agencies to misleading ad campaigns to companies who refuse to accept responsibility for years of damage, the airwaves are filled with deceit and hypocrisy. Most of the time, consumers must wade through the cesspool of "crap" they hear constantly. This kind of "hype" often complicates the buying decision because a client doesn't know if he or she is getting a straight answer.   [The internet has corrected some of this – because most of the time more information can lead to better decisions. It has also created a lot of "disinformation" for the customer to have to wade through]. Buyers must rely on sales consultants more than ever before to separate the facts from the fiction. That's where you come in.

Unfortunately, sales consultants are not immune from being swept up in the current of not always being forthcoming - particularly when a sale hangs in the balance. The temptation to lie, mislead or perhaps omit facts is great considering the competitive nature of the current marketplace. [It doesn't matter whether the salesperson is selling cars, houses, or even televisions]. Intentionally leaving a client with the wrong impression or making promises you have no intention of keeping will not build your business or secure brand loyalty. Inspired sellers run against the flow of loud-mouthed liars. Inspired sellers tell the truth - always.

Several years ago, I worked with a gentleman who was very good at lying to his customers. He would literally promise them anything just to make a sale. If the car wasn't running right, or had a big dent, he told them he would get it fixed [even when he knew he couldn't]. If it needed an extra key, he promised he would deliver. If they wanted a bigger discount, he told them he could get it. He was a constant thorn in the side of his employer, because lies were continually flowing from his lips. Even though he went from dealership to dealership, it didn't stop him from lying. Finally, he had burned so many bridges with so many places that no one would hire him.

Think of the value that the Bible places on truth – telling. Even in the Garden of Eden, God laid out the truth, knowing full well that Adam and Eve would be consumed by the lie of the serpent. God spoke truth without any pretense, or diplomacy or sugar-coating. He didn't beat around the bush, [no pun intended] – He just laid the facts in front of Adam and let Adam take the information even though it was going to cost a relationship.

When Moses needed help in settling disputes among the children of Israel, God told him to *"select from all the people able men, such as fear God, men of truth…"* [Ex.18:21 NASB]

Joshua told the children of Israel to *"fear the LORD, serve Him in sincerity and in truth …"* [Joshua 24:14 NASB]

When the woman whose son had died needed a miracle, she exclaimed to the prophet, *"Now by this I know that you are a man of God, and that the word of the LORD in your mouth is the truth."* [I Kings 17:24 NASB].

The New Testament also records a great deal about truth-telling. Jesus said that we would *"Know the truth and the truth would set us free"* [John 8:32 NASB]. He even declared that He was the embodiment of truth in John 14:6 – *"For I am the way, the truth and the life; no man comes to the Father but by me."*

The Apostle Paul echoed this sentiment when he encouraged the Ephesians to *"speak the truth in love."* [Eph. 4:15 NASB] Or to the church at Corinth, when he told them, *"When I was a child, I spoke as a child, I understood as a child, I thought as a child; but when I became a man, I put away childish things."* [I Cor. 13:11 NKJV]

Now, I am not suggesting that you carry truth-telling so far that it intentionally hurts someone else. In sales, a little tact can go a long way. What I am talking about is not selling your lips to the Devil just to make a sale. Be careful with what you say, so that you never have to eat your words.

So today, the truth is - *you must realize to become an inspired seller is that it involves truth-telling.* If a customer asks a question, and you don't know the answer – tell them that you don't know, but you will find out. Don't make stuff up. Don't tap-dance around something to save face. When you make a mistake; own it. Don't try to minimize what you may have said or done. Just tell the truth to the customer and trust the process to work. If you have to apologize for what might have happened – make it a genuine heartfelt apology. [Salespeople are good at faking apologies by saying that they are sorry, without really meaning it].

If you gloss over an issue or whitewash the responsibility for an error, then the customer feels devalued and unappreciated. Sometimes, all it takes to ease a customer's frustrations is to truly listen to their complaint. Let them vent if they need to. If you don't, believe me, they *will* take their business elsewhere. Inspired sellers tell the truth, even sometimes at the cost of a future sale.

Tell the truth. As far as the principle of being trustworthy goes, telling the truth and refusing to lie or mislead, goes a long, long way.

XXI.   A DREAM REALIZED

"Let us not become weary in doing good, for at the proper time we will reap a harvest if we do not give up." [Galatians 6:9 NIV]

I have always believed that when you do the right thing, God will see and reward you for it. The trouble is that just isn't true, not always. Most of the time, when the right thing gets done, it goes unnoticed by anyone. Many of us work and work and work, hoping to be applauded and cheered by those around us, but the days go by and all we hear is silence. No one recognizes. No one gives us a pat on the back. No one compliments us. No one ever seems to notice the constant, steady, dutiful labor we put in. The lack of fanfare can often make us wonder why we keep doing what we are doing. I mean, why do the right thing if we are never going to be acknowledged and rewarded for it? You can't tell me that thought has never once crossed your mind.

99

Think about the story of Joseph for a moment. He had a dream from God, and sharing that dream cost him. He was rejected and tormented by his brothers, tossed into a pit where he languished and then he was sold into slavery. Taken in chains to a foreign land, he was put on the auction block where he was bought by Potiphar. Facing a life of servitude, he worked hard. And then to complicate matters, he was tempted by the wife of his master for days and months on end. Denying her constant advances, he continued to do what was right. The result? He was tossed into prison where he spent years waiting for God to deliver him. [Eventually, God intervened, and he became the number two man in the nation, one of the greatest in Egypt]. But that deliverance by God took a while. In fact, it took a long, long time.

Imagine what prison life must have been like. The cold stone walls choked out the fresh air and sunlight. The stench of molded straw and diarrhea permeated every breath. Rats stealing the crumbs of food or nibbling on the decaying skin of dying prisoners. The wailing and moaning of human souls as the guards ignored the despair and misery around them. This was Joseph's world; his daily, constant existence. As he scrubbed and mopped up the vomit of a fellow inmate, or shared the morsels of a meal to a starving soul, he did what was right. As he bandaged the infected wounds of his companions, or comforted the dying, he stayed true. Each and every day, he made an unbearable environment, a little better.

Why? I think Joseph understood that God had to work on his character. There were leadership skills that he could only learn in the depths of the dark prison. Despite the darkness of his situation, Joseph knew and trusted that God was in control. He CHOSE to do what was right in a hundred little ways – every day. Soon, with God's help, he was running the prison.

Joseph did what was right, not because he knew he would be rewarded by anyone else. He did what was right because it was right.

The best leadership skills come when the light of day is barely seen. From the depths of despair, God reveals who we truly are. Will we continue to do what is right because it is right, or will we stop because we are not being rewarded and recognized?

We all have dreams that God plants in our hearts. The trouble is that in our society today, most of us want instant gratification. We expect to see immediate results. We want God to microwave those dreams like a bag of store bought popcorn. And when that doesn't happen, we complain and moan and gripe and quit on each other, and worse, we quit on God.

It strikes me that the Bible says as a teen, Joseph pleaded with his brothers to let him out of the pit. Young Joseph cried and wailed so much that his brothers couldn't stand it. They sold him into slavery just to get him to shut up. But look at older Joseph. Not once does it say that Joseph despaired or argued or railed about his circumstances. He took what God did in his life, and he trusted God to work on changing him for the better. Older Joseph is a completely different person than younger Joseph. There has been so much of a transformation that over a decade later when his brothers stand before him – they do not recognize him at all. God had changed him that much.

So here is what I want you to remember. The truth is this: Do what is right. If you have a job to do, do it to the best of your ability and stop doing it to be recognized. Let God reward you when he is ready. He will. You see, God never puts one of His dreams into our hearts without making it happen in His time. Keep working. Keep making your calls. Keep following the processes. Do what is right. Who knows, you might find that doing the right thing changes you completely. It did Joseph.

101

"I think being endowed with the ability to work in gold, or silver or to cut and set stones would have been pretty cool labor."

YOU ARE THE INSPIRED SALESPERSON

Then the LORD said to Moses, 2 "See, I have chosen Bezalel son of Uri, the son of Hur, of the tribe of Judah, 3 and I have filled him with the Spirit of God."
[Exodus 31:1-3 NIV]

Think for a moment about how the pages of scripture are filled with examples of simple hearts being used in great ways by God. Perhaps you can relate to a young man, named Joseph, who was thrown into a pit, and then rescued and used by God. David, who was the runt of his family, and yet, boldly defeated a giant named Goliath and became King. Or even the simple life of Jesus, who came and ministered to the poor, the oppressed, and the hurting. It doesn't take much reading of the Bible to discover that God prefers to use the heart of an ordinary person to show forth the extraordinary. That is the heartbeat of this book. That anyone can be the "inspired" person, just by being open to what God wants to accomplish in you and through you.

103

The very first mention of being inspired by God is found in the book of Exodus. This man's story is worth reflecting on. As Moses is preparing to lay the groundwork for the Tabernacle, God fills the heart of a simple servant. Bezalel, who is known as the son of Uri, the son of Hur from the tribe of Judah is filled with the Spirit of God. The Lord tells Moses, *"I have filled him with the Spirit of God,"* and has given him, *"wisdom, understanding, knowledge, and all kinds of skills."* [Ex. 31:3 NIV] In addition, the Bible tells us how those incredible qualities would manifest themselves in his life; *"to make artistic designs for work in gold, silver and bronze, 5 to cut and set stones, to work in wood, and to engage in all kinds of crafts."* [v.4]

Now, don't miss this: I think being endowed with the ability to work in gold, or silver or to cut and set stones would have been pretty cool labor. Imagine going to work each day and being able to pick up a tool and work with pure gold, or silver, cut a ruby or sapphire. Think about the skill needed to fashion wood or form bronze. Those craftsmanship skills would have been and what meticulous work that must have been. Every gem cut just right. Every beam carved just so. Every detail checked and then triple-checked. What a glorious job, being able to work with your hands to prepare the meeting place with God.

God empowered this young man to do work. He didn't give Bezalel wisdom or understanding about his family as great that would have been. God did not endow him with understanding about how to minister to the masses. Or even knowledge on how to generate wealth and power or a gifted tongue. God gave him a supernatural ability to do labor. God saw the value of what this young man could do with an open heart and with willing hands.

Did you notice what God gave to Bezalel first? It wasn't the abilities, as great as all those things were. It wasn't wisdom, or understanding, or knowledge that Bezalel received first. The very first thing this servant received was God's Spirit. *"I have filled him with the Spirit of God...*" [v. 3] God filled Bezalel with His own Spirit, with Himself. Perhaps that is why if you study the name of Bezalel you discover that in the Hebrew, his name means, "*in the shadow of God*".

And here is another great truth. The empowerment wasn't just for Bezalel's benefit only. The inspiration was to be used for the demonstrating of God to others. Every person in the nation of Israel was about to benefit from what God was doing in one simple heart willing to receive whatever God planted and then do the work God had called him to do.

So, what about you? I hope that the pages of this book have been used by God to inspire you. You can be everything God wants you to be. [Remember the tabernacle had never been built before – it was a big undertaking]. Whether you work in a small store or a huge conglomerate, the Heavenly Father is constantly looking for willing servants like Bezalel. Like you. He is looking for people He can work in and through to show Himself in new and great and glorious ways.

Remember the best is yet to come. You are an inspired salesperson. Yes, you.

ABOUT THE AUTHOR

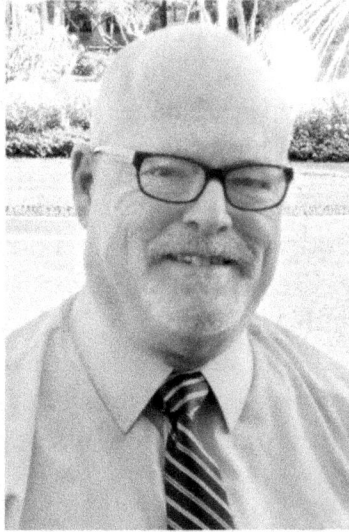

JAMES McMECHAN

With over 30 years of management and ministry experience, James has a passion to see people reach their God-given potential. He enjoys writing, traveling, and teaching people to realize and embrace the "heart" of God. He and his family currently reside in Mississippi.